# Brit Wit

The perfect riposte for every social occasion

Edited by Susie Jones

summersdale

**BRIT WIT**

## Condition of Sale

**Summersdale Publishers Ltd**
**46 West Street**
**Chichester**
**West Sussex**
**PO19 1RP**
**UK**

www.summersdale.com

### Disclaimer

Printed and bound in Great Britain

ISBN 1 84024 415 1

# EDITOR'S NOTE

Winston Churchill was recently voted the Greatest Briton of all time in a BBC poll. But was he the wittiest? Make up your own mind as *Brit Wit* explores the many facets of the great British sense of humour so peculiar to this island and often unfathomable to those off it. Interspersed with cutting contributions from 'traditional' wits such as Samuel Johnson are ribald ripostes from modern sources – comedians, television presenters and yes, even women. All of them unique, but all of them witty and typically British through their subtlety or cynicism. That is not to say that only the Brits have ever raised a wry smile. It was with great regret that Groucho Marx ('I never forget a face – but in your case I'll make an exception') and Dorothy Parker ('She runs the gamut of emotions from A to B', of Katharine Hepburn) had to stay out of this book!

So here you have it – the world with a pinch of salt. A Small Islander's guide to life, the universe and everything. Wow your friends, cow your enemies, and force yourself to see the funny side in a world that takes itself too seriously and not seriously enough. After all, as W. Somerset Maugham once observed, 'She had a pretty gift for quotation, which is a serviceable substitute for wit'.

Susie Jones

# Contents

# Brit Wit

# Quotes and Quotations

Find enough clever things to say, and you're a
Prime Minister; write them down and you're
a Shakespeare.
George Bernard Shaw, dramatist, literary critic and socialist
spokesman (1856-1950)

It is better to be quotable than to be honest.
Tom Stoppard, playwright

She had a pretty gift for quotation, which is a
serviceable substitute for wit.
W(illiam) Somerset Maugham, writer (1874-1965)

It is a good thing for an uneducated man to read books of quotations.
Winston Churchill, politician and statesman (1874-1965)

♋

A widely-read man never quotes accurately… misquotation is the pride and privilege of the learned.
Hesketh Pearson, actor, director and biographer (1887-1964)

♋

The nicest thing about quotes is that they give us a nodding acquaintance with the originator which is often socially impressive.
Kenneth Williams, actor and comic (1926-1988)

♋

You cram these words into mine ears against the stomach of my sense .
William Shakespeare, poet and playwright (1564-1616), *The Tempest*

Few of the many wise apothegms which have been uttered have prevented a single foolish action.

Thomas Babington Macaulay, historian and author (1800-1859)

♋

A facility for quotation covers the absence of original thought.

Dorothy L. Sayers, writer and theologian (1893-1957)

♋

I pick my favourite quotations and store them in my mind as ready armour, offensive or defensive, amid the struggle of this turbulent existence.

Robert Burns, poet (1759-1796)

# Insults

I fart in your general direction.
French soldier in *Monty Python and the Holy Grail*

♋

Your brain is like the four-headed man-eating haddock-fish beast of Aberdeen. It doesn't exist.
*Blackadder*

♋

What a tiresome affected sod.
Noel Coward, actor, dramatist and playwright (1899-1973) on Oscar Wilde

# Insults

Unreconstructed wankers.
Tony Blair, Prime Minister on the Scottish media, 1997

How tartly that gentleman looks! I never can see him but I am heart-burned an hour after.
William Shakespeare, *Much Ado About Nothing*

The haste of a fool is the slowest thing in the world.
Thomas Shadwell, dramatist and poet (c.1642-1692)

A stupid man's report of what a clever man says can never be accurate, because he unconsciously translates what he hears into something he can understand.
Bertrand Russell, author, mathematician and philosopher (1872-1970)

He is morally insensitive and aesthetically disgusting.
George Orwell, author (1903-1950) on Rudyard Kipling

O, she is the antidote to desire.
William Congreve, playwright (1670-1729), *The Way of the World*, 1700

A man who looks like a sexually confused, ageing hairdresser: the Teasy Weasy of Fleet Street.
Richard Littlejohn, journalist on Peregrine Worsthorne

Thou eunuch of language… thou pimp of gender… murderous accoucheur of infant learning… thou pickle-herring in the puppet show of nonsense.
Robert Burns on a critic

He owes his celebrity merely to his antiquity.
Lord Byron, poet (1788-1824) on Geoffrey Chaucer

Sir, you are like a pin, but without either its head or its point.
Douglas Jerrold, dramatist and writer (1803-1857)

♋

You look wise. Pray correct that error.
Charles Lamb, essayist and poet (1864-1945)

♋

He can't see a belt without hitting below it.
Margot Asquith, author (1864-1945) on David Lloyd George

# Insults

So boring you fall asleep halfway through her name.
Alan Bennett, dramatist, on Arianna Stassinopoulos

Is it always his desire to give his imitation of a semi-house-trained polecat?
Michael Foot, politician and journalist on Norman Tebbit

When they circumcised Herbert Samuel they threw away the wrong bit.
David Lloyd George, statesman (1863-1945)

Her face could launch a thousand dredgers.
Jack de Manio, radio broadcaster (1914-1988) on Glenda Jackson

♋

Lord Sandwich: Sir, you will die either of the pox or on the gallows
John Wilkes: Depending on whether I embrace your mistress or your principles

♋

'Tis such fools as you that makes the world full of ill-favour'd children.
William Shakespeare, *As You Like It*

Oh shut up Balders. You'd laugh at a Shakespeare comedy.
Rowan Atkinson, *Blackadder*

♋

No one can have a higher opinion of him than I have, and I think he's a dirty little beast.
W. S. Gilbert, librettist and author of comic operettas (1836-1911)

♋

He is an old bore. Even the grave yawns for him.
Herbert Beerbohm Tree, actor and theatrical producer (1853-1917) on Israel Zangwill

Thou whoreson zed! Thou unnecessary letter!
William Shakespeare, *King Lear*

♋

Of all the bulls that live, this hath the greatest
ass's ears.
Queen Elizabeth I (1533-1603)

♋

You beat your pate, and fancy wit will come;
Knock as you please, there's nobody at home.
Alexander Pope, writer and poet (1688-1744)

You're about as useful as a one-legged man at an arse-kicking contest.
Rowan Atkinson, *Blackadder*

☉

Leonardo DiCaprio is patently the result of an unnatural act of passion between William Hague and the piglet from *Babe*.
A. A. Gill, restaurant critic

☉

She is a peacock in everything but beauty.
Oscar Wilde, *The Picture of Dorian Gray*

☉

Like the British Constitution, she owes her success in practice to her inconsistencies in principle.
Thomas Hardy, novelist (1840-1928)

# Ripostes

A fly, sir, may sting a stately horse, and make him wince; but one is but an insect, and the other is a horse still.
Samuel Johnson, author and critic (1709-1784)

🦀

God forgive you, but I never can.
Queen Elizabeth I to the Countess of Nottingham

🦀

Your wit's too hot, it speeds too fast, 'twill tire.
William Shakespeare, *Love's Labour's Lost*

One wit, like a knuckle ham in soup, gives a zest and flavour to the dish, but more than one serves only to spoil the pottage.
Tobias George Smollett, novelist (1721-1771)

♋

I refuse to answer that question on the grounds that I don't know the answer.
Douglas Adams, author (1952-2001)

♋

You may be as vicious about me as you please. You will only do me justice.
Richard Burton, actor (1925-1984)

# Work and Money

I won't eat anything that has intelligent life, but I'd gladly eat a network executive or a politician.
Marty Feldman, writer, comedian and actor (1933-1982)

How long was I in the army? Five foot eleven.
Spike Milligan, comedian (1918-2002)

Comedy, like sodomy, is an unnatural act.
Marty Feldman

## Work and Money

And the back of his anorak was leaping up and down, and people were chucking money to him. I said 'Do you earn a living doing that?' He said 'Yes, this is my livelihood'.
Tommy Cooper, comedian (1922-1984)

Victoria looks like a bouncer in a nightclub. 'Can't go in there, mate, I'm the Queen. Look at that penny, that's me on there. Go on, clear off'.
Paul Merton, comedian

Civil servants – no longer servants, no longer civil.
Winston Churchill

There are many vampires in the world today -
you only have to think of the film business.
Christopher Lee, actor

The Army Selection Board told me I had the
voice of a gentleman and the spelling of a
clown. What spelling had to do with winning
wars is beyond me.
Oliver Reed, actor (1939-1999)

I'm a skilled, professional actor. Whether or
not I've any talent is beside the point.
Michael Caine, actor

Well, we can't stand around here doing
nothing, people will think we're workmen.
Spike Milligan

♋

Politics is perhaps the only profession for
which no preparation is thought necessary.
Robert Louis Stevenson, novelist and poet (1850-1894)

♋

If life were fair, Dan Quayle would be making
a living asking 'Do you want fries with that?'
John Cleese, comedian and actor

Advertising is legalised lying.
H. G. Wells, novelist, journalist, sociologist and historian (1866-1946)

♋

The ability to foretell what is going to happen tomorrow, next week, next month, and next year. And to have the ability afterwards to explain why it didn't happen.
Winston Churchill on what qualities a politician required

♋

The first thing we do, let's kill all the lawyers.
William Shakespeare, *Henry VI Part II*

If you can't get a job as a pianist in a brothel you become a royal reporter.
Max Hastings

ᅇ

I have learned from experience that, in the bluff and counterbluff of world politics, to draw a hostile war lord as a horrible monster is to play his game. What he doesn't like is being shown as a silly ass.
David Lowe on being a political cartoonist

ᅇ

People expect the clergy to have the grace of a swan, the friendliness of a sparrow, the strength of an eagle and the night hours of an owl - and some people expect such a bird to live on the food of a canary.
Edward Jeffrey, clergyman

I expect you'll be becoming a schoolmaster sir.
That's what most of the gentlemen does sir,
that gets sent down for indecent behaviour.
Evelyn Waugh, satirical novelist (1903-1966)

၏

I love deadlines. I especially like the whooshing
sound they make as they go flying by.
Douglas Adams

၏

One of the symptoms of an approaching
nervous breakdown is the belief that one's
work is terribly important.
Bertrand Russell

Nowher so bisy a man as he ther nas,
And yet he semed bisier than he was.
Geoffrey Chaucer, father of English literature (1343-1400), *The Clerk's Tale*

☟

I like work: it fascinates me. I can sit and look at it for hours.
Jerome K. Jerome, humour writer (1859-1927)

☟

Term, holidays, term, holidays, till we leave school, and then work, work, work till we die.
C. S. Lewis, author (1898-1963), *Surprised by Joy*, 1954

Every man loves what he is good at.
Thomas Shadwell

℅

The discipline of colleges and universities is in general contrived, not for the benefit of the students, but for the interest, or more properly speaking, for the ease of the masters.
Adam Smith, economist and philosopher (1723-1790)

℅

Asking a working writer what he thinks about critics is like asking a lamppost how it feels about dogs.
Christopher Hampton, screenplay writer

Nothing is really work unless you would
rather be doing something else.
James M. Barrie, writer (1860-1937)

♋

Punctuality is the virtue of the bored.
Evelyn Waugh, *Diaries of Evelyn Waugh,* 1976

♋

I find it rather easy to portray a businessman.
Being bland, rather cruel and incompetent
comes naturally to me.
John Cleese

The commercial class has always mistrusted verbal brilliancy and wit, deeming such qualities, perhaps with some justice, frivolous and unprofitable.

Dorothy Nevill, writer (1826-1913)

It was such a lovely day I thought it a pity to get up.

W. Somerset Maugham

My neighbour asked if he could use my lawnmower and I told him of course he could, so long as he didn't take it out of my garden.

Eric Morecambe, comedian

Time is an illusion, lunchtime doubly so.
Douglas Adams

♋

Make lots of money. Enjoy the work. Operate within the law. Choose any two of three.
Jack Dee, comedian

♋

Idleness is only a coarse name for my infinite capacity for living in the present.
Cyril Connolly, journalist and editor (1903-1974)

...skewered through and through with office-pens, and bound hand and foot with red tape.
Charles Dickens, writer (1812-1870), *David Copperfield* 1849-1850

♋

Everybody was saying we must have more leisure. Now they are complaining they are unemployed.
Prince Philip, Duke of Edinburgh

♋

Every man is a potential genius until he does something.
Herbert Beerbohm Tree

The dullard's envy of brilliant men is always assuaged by the suspicion that they will come to a bad end.
Max Beerbohm, writer and caricaturist (1872-1956)

♋

Work is not always required. There is such a thing as sacred idleness.
George MacDonald, novelist and poet (1824-1905)

♋

Dark forces dragged me away from the keyboard, swirling forces of irresistible intensity and power.
Boris Johnson, politician, his excuse for missing deadlines

I have always been a grumbler. I am designed for the part – sagging face, weighty underlip, rumbling, resonant voice. Money couldn't buy a better grumbling outfit.

J. B. Priestley, novelist (1894-1984)

♋

All I ask is the chance to prove that money can't make me happy.

Spike Milligan

♋

And God said, 'Let there be light'; and there was light, but the Electricity Board said He would have to wait until Thursday to be connected. And God saw the light and it was good; He saw the quarterly bill and that was not good.

Spike Milligan

People say I wasted my money. I say 90 percent went on women, fast cars, and booze. The rest I wasted.
George Best, footballer

Borrow fivers off everyone.
Richard Branson, businessman and multi-millionaire in answer to the question: What is the quickest way to become a millionaire?

To be clever enough to get all the money, one must be stupid enough to want it.
G. K. Chesterton, author (1874-1936)

Brit Wit

A wise man will live as much within his wit as within his income.
Lord Chesterfield, politician (1694-1773)

෨

I told the Inland Revenue I didn't owe them a penny because I lived near the seaside.
Ken Dodd, comedian

෨

There are three ways of losing money: racing is the quickest, women the most pleasant, and farming the most certain.
Lord Amherst, army officer (1717-1797)

# Work and Money

Anyone who lives within their means suffers
from a lack of imagination.
Attributed to Oscar Wilde

♋

Lack of money is the root of all evil.
George Bernard Shaw

♋

There's no money in poetry, but then there's
no poetry in money, either.
Robert Graves, poet and novelist (1895-1985)

We may see the small value God has for riches, by the people he gives them to.
Alexander Pope, *Thoughts on Various Subjects*, 1727

People don't resent having nothing nearly as much as too little.
Ivy Compton-Burnett, writer (1884-1969)

One man's wage increase is another man's price increase.
Harold Wilson, former Prime Minister (1916-1995)

# Work and Money

'It was as true,' said Mr Barkis, '… as taxes is. And nothing's truer than them.'
Charles Dickens, *David Copperfield*

🦀

I'm as poor as a church mouse, that's just had an enormous tax bill on the very day his wife ran off with another mouse, taking all the cheese.
Edmund, *Blackadder*

🦀

All money nowadays seems to be produced with a natural homing instinct for the Treasury.
Prince Philip, Duke of Edinburgh

The only thing I like about rich people is their money.
Nancy Astor, politician (1879-1964)

Nothing except the mint can make money without advertising.
Thomas Babington Macaulay

I used to empty ashtrays for the cigarette butts, re-roll them and make myself a fag. I used to live on a pound of sausages and a cooking apple.
Glenda Jackson, actress

# Work and Money

Anyone who says that money can't buy you happiness is putting out propaganda for the rich.
Michael Caine

I told the players we need to win so that I can have the cash to buy some new ones...
Chris Turner, Peterborough manager, before Peterborough played Middlesborough in the League Cup Quarter-final

Economy is going without something you do want in case you should, some day, want something you probably won't want.
Anthony Hope Hawkins, novelist and playwright (1863-1933)

Money can't buy poverty.
Marty Feldman

☙

The difference between English and American humour is $150 a minute.
Eric Idle, comedian

☙

All decent people live beyond their incomes nowadays, and those who aren't respectable live beyond other people's. A few gifted individuals manage to do both.
Saki, aka Hector Hugo Munro, short story writer (1870-1916)

☙

I've had to swap my Merc for a BMW, I'm down to my last 37 suits and I'm drinking non-vintage champagne.
Ron Atkinson, sports commentator after being sacked by Manchester United in 1986

# Work and Money

I'd hang myself, but we can't afford the rope.
Hamilton Academicals'Iain Munro, footballer

♋

The only reason I made a commercial for American Express was to pay for my American Express bill.
Peter Ustinov, actor and writer (1921-2004)

♋

We all need money, but there are degrees of desperation.
Anthony Burgess, novelist, composer and critic (1917-1993)

♋

When an actor comes to me and wants to discuss his character, I say, 'It's in the script.' If he says, 'But what's my motivation?' I say, 'Your salary.'
Alfred Hitchcock, director (1899-1980)

# Advice

A sure cure for seasickness is to sit under a tree.
Spike Milligan

♋

So I was getting into my car, and this bloke says to me 'Can you give me a lift?' I said 'Sure, you look great, the world's your oyster, go for it.'
Tommy Cooper

♋

Never put a sock in a toaster.
Eddie Izzard, comedian

# Advice

Never stand so high upon a principle that you cannot lower it to suit the circumstances.
Winston Churchill

♋

Contraceptives should be used on every conceivable occasion.
Spike Milligan

♋

Build a man a fire, and he'll be warm for a day. Set a man on fire, and he'll be warm for the rest of his life.
Terry Pratchett, author

A little inaccuracy sometimes saves tons of explanation.
Saki

♋

Never keep up with the Joneses. Drag them down to your level. It's cheaper.
Quentin Crisp, author (1908-1999)

♋

Human beings, who are almost unique in having the ability to learn from the experience of others, are also remarkable for their apparent disinclination to do so.
Douglas Adams

♋

# Advice

I always pass on good advice. It's the only thing to do with it. It is never any use to oneself.
Oscar Wilde, *An Ideal Husband*

If you're going to make rubbish, be the best rubbish in it.
Richard Burton

It's okay to let yourself go, just as long as you let yourself back.
Mick Jagger, musician

Bear in mind the simple rule, X squared to the power of two minus five over the seven point eight three times nineteen is approximately equal to the cube root of MCC squared divided by X minus a quarter of a third percent. Keep that in mind, and you can't go very far wrong.
Eric Idle

♋

Good advice is always certain to be ignored, but that's no reason not to give it.
Agatha Christie, author (1890-1976)

♋

The men who really believe in themselves are all in lunatic asylums.
G. K. Chesteron

# Advice

I always advise people never to give advice.
P. G. Wodehouse, writer (1881-1975)

ᏮᏯ

One should only see a psychiatrist out of boredom.
Muriel Spark, novelist and satirist

ᏮᏯ

In university they don't tell you that the greater part of the law is learning to tolerate fools.
Doris Lessing, writer

ᏮᏯ

Success is a great deodorant. It takes away all your past smells.
Elizabeth Taylor, actress

# Politics

The best argument against democracy is a five-minute conversation with the average voter.
Winston Churchill

🦀

In war, you can only be killed once, but in politics, many times.
Winston Churchill

🦀

In politics, if you want anything said, ask a man. If you want something done, ask a woman.
Margaret Thatcher, former Prime Minister

Politicians. Little tin gods on wheels.
Rudyard Kipling, writer (1865-1936)

The difference between a misfortune and a calamity? If Gladstone fell into the Thames, it would be a misfortune. But if someone dragged him out again, it would be a calamity.
Benjamin Disraeli, statesman (1804-1881)

A Conservative Government is an organised hypocrisy.
Benjamin Disraeli

Finality is not the language of politics.
Benjamin Disraeli

ஓ

A Foreign Secretary is forever poised between
the cliché and the indiscretion.
Harold MacMillan, former Prime Minister (1894-1986),
comment made in Parliament

ஓ

I never meant to say that the Conservatives
are generally stupid. I meant to say that stupid
people are generally Conservative. I believe
that is so obviously and universally admitted a
principle that I hardly think any gentleman will
deny it.
John Stuart Mill, philosopher (1806-1873) *Letter (to Conservative
MP Sir John Pilkington)*, March 1866

Politics

Laws are generally found to be nets of such a texture, as the little creep through, the great break through, and the middle-sized are alone entangled in.
William Shenstone, poet (1714-1763), *Essays on Men, Manners, and Things*

♋

There is no art which one government sooner learns of another than that of draining money from the pockets of the people.
Adam Smith

♋

Tory and Whig in turns shall be my host, I taste no politics in boil'd and roast.
Revd Sydney Smith, clergyman (1771-1845) to John Murray

Politics are usually the executive expression of human immaturity.
Vera Brittain, writer (1893-1970)

When I call for statistics about the rate of infant mortality, what I want is proof that fewer babies died when I was Prime Minister than when anyone else was Prime Minister. That is a political statistic.
Winston Churchill

They are nothing else but a load of kippers – two-faced, with no guts.
Eric Heffer, former Labour MP (1922-1991) on the Conservative Government

Despotism tempered by assassination.
Lord Reith, first Director General of the BBC (1889-1971) on the best form of government

Euphemisms are unpleasant truths wearing diplomatic cologne.
Quentin Crisp

♋

We know what happens to people who stay in the middle of the road. They get run over.
Aneurin Bevan, politician (1897-1960)

♋

Being an MP is the sort of job all working class parents want for their children – clean, indoors and no heavy lifting.
Dianne Abbott, politician

♋

The House of Commons is the longest running farce in the West End.
Cyril Smith, politician

If Kitchener is not a great man, he is, at least, a great poster.
Margot Asquith

🦀

Listening to a speech by [Neville] Chamberlain is like paying a visit to Woolworths; everything in its place and nothing over sixpence.
Anuerin Bevan

🦀

Call that a maiden speech? I call that a brazen hussy of a speech.
Winston Churchill to A. P. Herbert

🦀

She can't see an institution without hitting it with her handbag.
Julian Critchley, politician and journalist on Margaret Thatcher

The less people know about what is really going on, the easier it is to wield power and authority.
Prince Charles

🦀

The ultimate result of shielding men from the effects of folly is to fill the world with fools.
Herbert Spencer, philosopher (1820-1903)

🦀

Standing in the middle of the road is very dangerous; you get knocked down by the traffic from both sides.
Margaret Thatcher

🦀

Tony Blair puts two poems in a bus shelter and calls it a university.
Victoria Wood, comedy writer

The President is a cross-eyed Texan warmonger, unelected, inarticulate, who epitomises the arrogance of American foreign policy.
Boris Johnson on George W. Bush

Tony Blair is a mixture of Harry Houdini and a greased piglet. He is barely human in his elusiveness. Nailing Blair is like trying to pin jelly to a wall.
Boris Johnson

We started trying to set up a small anarchist community, but the people wouldn't obey the rules.
Alan Bennett

We all know that Prime Ministers are wedded to the truth, but like other married couples they sometimes live apart.
Saki

༄

The Labour Party has lost the last four elections. If they lose another, they get to keep the Liberal Party.
Clive Anderson, entertainer

༄

If liberty means anything at all, it means the right to tell people what they don't want to hear.
George Orwell, author (1903-1950)

༄

[She has turned] the British bulldog into a Reagan poodle.
David Steel, politician on Margaret Thatcher

The Minister of Transport issued this appeal to motorists: Can anyone give him a lift to Leicester?
Eric Idle

By concentrating on what is good in people, by appealing to their idealism and their sense of justice, and by asking them to put their faith in the future, socialists put themselves at a severe disadvantage.
Ian McEwan, author

Politics is the enemy of the imagination.
Ian McEwan

Democracy means government by the uneducated, while aristocracy means government by the badly educated.
G. K. Chesterton

# Sport

Sudden success in golf is like the sudden acquisition of wealth. It is apt to unsettle and deteriorate the character.
P. G. Wodehouse

I became a great runner because if you're a kid in Leeds and your name is Sebastian you've got to become a great runner.
Sebastian Coe, athlete

The only athletic sport I ever mastered was backgammon.
Douglas Jerrold

Ally MacLeod thinks that tactics are a new kind of mint.
Billy Connolly, comedian, on infamous Scotland soccer manager Ally McLeod

♋

When I first met him [David Beckham] I didn't know whether to shake his hand or lick his face.
Robbie Williams, musician

♋

Oh God! If there be cricket in heaven let there also be rain.
Alec Douglas-Home, politician (1903-1995)

♋

The Oxford rowing crew – eight minds with but a single thought, if that.
Max Beerbohm

# Sport

The place of the father in the modern suburban family is a very small one, particularly if he plays golf.
Bertrand Russell

ೞ

That's great, tell him he's Pelé and get him back on.
John Lambie, Partick Thistle manager, when told a concussed striker did not know who he was

ೞ

Golf, like measles, should be caught young.
P. G. Wodehouse

ೞ

I regard golf as an expensive way of playing marbles.
G. K. Chesterton

Golf is a day spent in a round of strenuous idleness.
William Wordsworth, poet (1770-1850)

♋

I don't make mistakes. I make prophesies which immediately turn out to be wrong.
Murray Walker, the Voice of Formula One

♋

Baseball has the great advantage over cricket of being sooner ended.
George Bernard Shaw

# Sport

Serious sport has nothing to do with fair play. It is bound up with hatred, jealousy, boastfulness, disregard of all rules and sadistic pleasure in witnessing violence. In other words, it is war minus the shooting.
George Orwell

♋

I'd hate to be next door to her on her wedding night.
Peter Ustinov on Monica Seles

♋

Michael Chang has all the fire and passion of a public service announcement, so much so that he makes Pete Sampras appear fascinating.
Alf Ramsey, former England manager (1920-1999)

One way to stop a runaway horse is to bet on him.
Jeffrey Bernard, musician

ॐ

I'd rather be a footballer than an existentialist.
Robert Smith of The Cure

ॐ

They are a young side. It's like when you were eighteen with three girlfriends. The more you play, the more you learn.
Notts County's Mick Walker

ॐ

In my opinion cricket is too great a game to think about statistically.
E. H. Hendren, cricket player (1881-1962)

# Sport

I'm confident they play the game in heaven.
Wouldn't be heaven otherwise, would it?
Patrick Moore, astronomer, on cricket

♋

Personally, I have always looked on cricket as
organised loafing.
William Temple, former Archbishop of Canterbury (1881-1944)

♋

Look, if you're in the penalty area and aren't
quite sure what to do with the ball, just stick it
in the net and we'll discuss all your options
afterwards.
Attributed to Bill Shankly, footballer and manager, to player

♋

Cricket is a game which the British, not being
a spiritual people, had to invent in order to
have some concept of eternity.
Lord Mancroft, politician

It's a funny kind of month, October. For the really keen cricket fan it's when you discover that your wife left you in May.
Dennis Norden, entertainer

♋

Rugby is a good occasion for keeping thirty bullies far from the centre of the city.
Attributed to Oscar Wilde

♋

We've lost seven of our last eight matches. Only team that we've beaten was Western Samoa. Good job we didn't play the whole of Samoa.
Gareth Davies, rugby player, on the Welsh rugby team's performance

# Sport

In 1823, William Webb Ellis first picked up the ball in his arms and ran with it. And for the next 156 years forwards have been trying to work out why.
Tasker Watkins, President of the Welsh Rugby Union

It's not in support of cricket but as an earnest protest against golf.
Max Beerbohm when asked to contribute to W. G. Grace's testimonial

Jogging is for people who aren't intelligent enough to watch television.
Victoria Wood

I once jogged to the ashtray.
Will Self, novelist, when asked by *The Idler* if he had ever had any encounters with sport and exercise

♋

How do I view United? Preferably on television, but unfortunately we have to go down the East Lancs Road and get a bit closer.
Howard Kendall, boss of Everton

♋

Preston. They're one of my old clubs. But then most of them are. I've had more clubs than Jack Nicklaus.
Tommy Docherty, football manager

♋

I tend to believe that cricket is the greatest thing that God ever created on earth... certainly greater than sex, although sex isn't too bad either.
Harold Pinter, dramatist

# Foreigners

We have really everything in common with America nowadays except, of course, language.
Oscar Wilde, *The Canterville Ghost*, 1882

Everybody has a right to pronounce foreign names as he chooses.
Winston Churchill

German is the most extravagantly ugly language. It sounds like someone using a sick bag on a 747.
Willy Rushton, comedian (1937-1996)

♋

Perhaps we can at least teach the Americans that there are better things to do with a cigar than Clinton seems to realise.
Auberon Waugh, writer and journalist (1940-2001)

♋

That kind of patriotism which consists in hating all other nations.
Mrs Gaskell, *Sylvia's Lovers,* 1863

♋

The best thing I know between France and England is – the sea.
Douglas Jerrold regarding The Anglo-French Alliance

# Foreigners

You must consider every man your enemy who speaks ill of your king: and... you must hate a Frenchman as you hate a devil.
Horatio Nelson, British naval officer (1758-1805)

I look upon Switzerland as an inferior sort of Scotland.
Revd Sydney Smith

Abroad is unutterably bloody and foreigners are fiends.
Nancy Mitford, author (1904-1973) *The Pursuit of Love,* 1945

I grew up in Europe, where the history comes from.
Eddie Izzard

The 100% American is 99% idiot.
George Bernard Shaw

꩜

I am quite serious when I say that I do not believe there are, on the whole earth besides, so many intensified bores as in these United States. No man can form an adequate idea of the real meaning of the word, without coming here.
Charles Dickens

꩜

I do not know the American gentleman, God forgive me for putting two such words together.
Charles Dickens

Holland is so low it is saved only by being dammed.
Thomas Hood, poet (1799-1845)

The United States, I believe, are under the impression that they are twenty years in advance of this country; whilst, as a matter of actual verifiable fact, of course, they are just about six hours behind it.
Harold Hobson, novelist, *The Devil in Woodford Wells,* 1946

I have just been to Naples to see Vesuvius and would you believe it the bloody fools have let it go out.
Spike Milligan

I hate the French because they are all slaves and wear wooden shoes.
Oliver Goldsmith, poet (1728-1774), *Essays (24 (1765 ed.))*, appeared in the *British Magazine*, June, 1760

♋

I speak Esparanto like a native.
Spike Milligan

♋

American is the language in which people say what they mean as Italian is the language in which they say what they feel. English is the language in which what a character means or feels has to be deduced from what he or she says, which may be quite the opposite.
John Mortimer, playwright and novelist, *Mail on Sunday*, 1989

Every times Europe looks across the Atlantic to see the American eagle, it observes only the rear end of an ostrich.
H. G. Wells

♋

Realising that they will never be a world power, the Cypriots have decided to settle for being a world nuisance.
George Mikes, writer

♋

*Robin and Marian* was supposed to be called *The Death of Robin Hood* but Americans don't like heroes who die or anything that might smack of not being a victory.
Sean Connery, actor

There are no unemployed in Russia or in Dartmoor jail, and for the same reason.
Philip Snowden, politician

୭

Los Angeles is awful – like Liverpool with palm trees.
Johnny Rotten, musician

୭

Americans have different ways of saying things. They say 'elevator', we say 'lift'... they say 'President', we say 'stupid psychopathic git'.
Alexi Sayle, comedian

୭

I have just been all round the world and have formed a very poor opinion of it.
Thomas Beecham, composer (1879-1961)

My pictures always seem to be filmed in places that I can't pronounce.
Roger Moore, actor

♋

What a pity, when Christopher Columbus discovered America, that he ever mentioned it.
Margot Asquith

♋

So is eating frogs, cruelty to geese and urinating in the street. But that's no reason to inflict it on the rest of us.
Rowan Atkinson on the French, *Blackadder*

He is the only bull I know who carries his own china closet with him.
Winston Churchill on US Secretary of State John Foster Dulles

♋

The British tourist is always happy abroad as long as the natives are waiters.
Robert Morley, actor (1908-1992)

♋

When Frenchmen are talking, never lift the needle off the gramophone: it only goes back to the beginning.
Oliver Lyttelton, army officer and politician (1893-1972)

♋

One man's Mede is another man's Persian.
Saki

Everyone's too nice – no wonder Gary Lineker went there.
Noel Gallagher, musician, on Japan

☞

You can get far in North America with laconic grunts. 'Huh,' 'hun,' and 'hi!' in their various modulations, together with 'sure,' 'guess so,' 'that so?' and 'nuts!' will meet almost any contingency.
Ian Fleming, writer (1908-1964)

☞

A plenitude of peanut butter and a dearth of hot mustard.
Patrick Dean, former British Ambassador to the US, on American cuisine

On my first day in New York a guy asked me if I knew where Central Park was. When I told him I didn't he said, 'Do you mind if I mug you here?'
Paul Merton

☊

All my wife has ever taken from the Mediterranean – from that whole vast intuitive culture – are four bottles of Chianti to make into lamps, and two china condiment donkeys labelled Sally and Peppy.
Peter Shaffer, playwright

# Religion

The Bible tells us to love our neighbours, and also to love our enemies; probably because generally they are the same people.
G. K. Chesterton

♋

To the philosophical eye the vices of the clergy are far less dangerous than their virtues.
Edward Gibbon, historian (1737-1794), *The Decline and Fall of the Roman Empire,* 1776-1788

♋

Heresy is another word for freedom of thought.
Graham Greene, writer (1904-1991)

It may be that our role on this planet is not to worship God, but to create him.
Arthur C. Clarke, writer

෨

As the French say, there are three sexes – men, women and clergymen.
Revd Sydney Smith

෨

An atheist is a man who has no invisible means of support.
John Buchan, author (1875-1940)

෨

There is not in the universe a more ridiculous, nor a more contemptible animal, than a proud clergyman.
Henry Fielding, novelist (1707-1754)

# Religion

In the beginning the Universe was created. This has made a lot of people very angry and is widely regarded as a bad move.
Douglas Adams

♋

Astrology proves one scientific fact, and one only; there's one born every minute.
Patrick Moore

♋

I don't believe in astrology. The only stars I can blame for my failures are those that walk about the stage.
Noel Coward

What would I like the sermon to be about, vicar? I would like it to be about 10 minutes.
Arthur Wellesley, politician (1769-1852)

♋

We have not lost faith, but we have transferred it from God to the Medical profession.
George Bernard Shaw

♋

It is the test of a good religion whether you can joke about it.
G. K. Chesterton

♋

When people cease to believe in God, they don't believe in nothing, they believe in anything.
G. K. Chesterton

We make guilty of our disasters the sun, the moon, and the stars: as if we were villains by necessity; fools by heavenly compulsion.
William Shakespeare, *King Lear*

♋

The New Testament is basically about what happened when God got religion.
Terry Pratchett

♋

People are too apt to treat God as if he were a minor royalty.
Herbert Beerbohm Tree

Man is made to adore and to obey: but if you will not command him, if you give him nothing to worship, he will fashion his own divinities, and find a chieftain in his own passions.
Benjamin Disraeli

For what a man would like to be true, that he more readily believes.
Francis Bacon, philosopher (1561-1626)

Religion is something left over from the infancy of our intelligence, it will fade away as we adopt reason and science as our guidelines.
Bertrand Russell

Religion to me has always been the wound, not the bandage.
Dennis Potter, playwright (1935-1994)

Her conception of God was certainly not orthodox. She felt towards Him as she might have felt towards a glorified sanitary engineer; and in some of her speculations she seems hardly to distinguish between the Deity and the Drain.
Lytton Strachey, biographer (1880-1932) on Florence Nightingale

Not a religion for gentlemen.
King Charles II on Presbyterianism

Christians have burnt each other, quite persuaded
That all the Apostles would have done as they did.
Lord Byron

🦀

An honest God's the noblest work of man.
Samuel Butler, author (1835-1902)

🦀

You never see animals going through the absurd and often horrible fooleries of magic and religion. Only man behaves with such gratuitous folly. It is the price he has to pay for being intelligent but now, as yet, intelligent enough.
Aldous Huxley, novelist (1894-1963)

When I told the people of Northern Ireland that I was an atheist, a woman in the audience stood up and said, 'Yes, but is it the God of the Catholics or the God of the Protestants in whom you don't believe?'
Quentin Crisp

♋

The fact that a believer is happier than a sceptic is no more to the point than the fact that a drunken man is happier than a sober one.
George Bernard Shaw

♋

The Puritan hated bear-baiting, not because it gave pain to the bear, but because it gave pleasure to the spectators.
Thomas Babington Macaulay

Roses are reddish
Violets are bluish
If it weren't for Christmas
We'd all be Jewish.
Benny Hill, comedian (1924-1992)

People may say what they like about the decay of Christianity; the religious system that produced green Chartreuse can never really die.
Saki

It's Life that defeats the Christian Church. She's always well-equipped to deal with Death.
Joe Orton, author (1933-1967), *The Erpingham Camp*, 1967

# Religion

'God knows how you Protestants can be expected to have any sense of direction,' she said. 'It's different with us. I haven't been to mass for years, I've got every mortal sin on my conscience, but I know when I'm doing wrong. I'm still a Catholic.'
Angus Wilson, novelist (1913-1991)

Metaphysical speculation is about as pointless as a discussion on the meaning of one's lungs. They're for breathing.
P. D. James, novelist

God is a gentleman. He prefers blondes.
Joe Orton, *Loot*, 1966

# Vices and Virtues

Virtue is like a rich stone, best plain set.
Francis Bacon, *Of Beauty*, 1597

♋

I hate people who think it's clever to take drugs... like custom officers.
Jack Dee

♋

I have often wished I had time to cultivate modesty. But I am too busy thinking about myself.
Dame Edith Sitwell, poet (1887-1964)

# Vices and Virtues

If one sticks too rigidly to one's principles, one would hardly see anybody.
Agatha Christie

♋

I'm not against the police, I'm just afraid of them.
Alfred Hitchcock

♋

The only way to get rid of a temptation is to yield to it.
Oscar Wilde, The Picture of Dorian Gray

♋

Minds, like bodies, will often fall into a pimpled, ill-conditioned state from mere excess of comfort.
Charles Dickens

Subdue your appetites, my dears, and you've conquered human nature.
Charles Dickens

♋

Vices are sometimes only virtues carried to excess!
Charles Dickens

♋

Follow your inclinations with due regard to the policeman round the corner.
W. Somerset Maugham, *Of Human Bondage*, 1915

No one gossips about other people's secret virtues.
Bertrand Russell

♋

The people who are regarded as moral luminaries are those who forego ordinary pleasures and find compensation in interfering with the pleasures of others.
Bertrand Russell

♋

Thieves respect property. They merely wish the property to become their property that they may more perfectly respect it.
G. K. Chesterton

I believe in getting into hot water; it keeps you clean.
G. K. Chesterton

People who can't be witty exert themselves to be devout and affectionate.
George Eliot, author (1819-1880)

The best car safety device is a rear-view mirror with a cop in it.
Dudley Moore, actor (1935-2002)

All charming people have something to conceal, usually their total dependence on the appreciation of others.
Cyril Connolly

I don't have a drug problem. I have a police problem.
Keith Richards, musician

🦀

The unfortunate thing about this world is that the good habits are much easier to give up than the bad ones.
W. Somerset Maugham

🦀

I'm into pop because I want to get rich, get famous and get laid.
Bob Geldof, musician

🦀

Let us have wine and women,
Mirth and laughter.
Sermons and soda-water the day after.
Lord Byron

And oftentimes excusing of a fault,
Doth make the fault the worse by the excuse.
William Shakespeare, *King John*

♋

You can't learn too soon that the most useful
thing about a principle is that it can always be
sacrificed to expediency.
W. Somerset Maugham

♋

Cynicism is the humour of hatred.
Herbert Beerbohm Tree

♋

Civilised men arrived in the Pacific armed with
alcohol, syphilis, trousers and the Bible.
Havelock Ellis, psychologist (1859-1939)

# Vices and Virtues

Scandal is gossip made tedious by morality.
Oscar Wilde, *Lady Windemere's Fan*

ॐ

Some rise by sin, and some by virtue fall.
William Shakespeare, *Measure for Measure*

ॐ

They say, best men are moulded out of faults,
And, for the most, become much more the better,
For being a little bad.
William Shakespeare, *Measure for Measure*

ॐ

I was horrified to find the other week that my second son is taking drugs. My very best ones too.
Bob Monkhouse, comedian (1928-2003)

He has all the virtues I dislike and none of the vices I admire.
Winston Churchill on Sir Stafford Cripps

♋

Commit the oldest sins, the newest kind of ways.
William Shakespeare, *Henry IV Part II*

♋

Her virtue was that she said what she thought, her vice that what she thought didn't amount to much.
Peter Ustinov

♋

I have come to regard the law-courts not as a cathedral but rather as a casino.
Richard Ingrams, journalist

# Writing, Publishing and Media

Only a mediocre writer is always at his best.
W. Somerset Maugham

♋

Some editors are failed writers, but so are most writers.
T. S. Eliot, poet (1888-1965)

♋

There are books of which the backs and covers are by far the best parts.
Charles Dickens

This paperback is very interesting, but I find it will never replace a hardcover book – it makes a very poor doorstop.
Alfred Hitchcock

♋

I once put 'exclusive' on the weather by mistake.
Piers Morgan, journalist and editor

♋

One always tends to overpraise a long book, because one has got through it.
E. M. Forster, novelist (1879-1970)

The last time I was in Spain I got through six Jeffrey Archer novels. I must remember to take enough toilet paper next time.
Bob Monkhouse

☙

The more I read him, the less I wonder that they poisoned him.
Thomas Babington Macaulay on Socrates

☙

Whenever I want a good read I get one of Jeffrey's novels, and stand on it, so I can reach the good books.
Steven Norris, politician, on Jeffrey Archer

The work of a queasy undergraduate scratching his pimples.
Virginia Woolf, author (1882-1941}, on *Ulysses* by James Joyce

♋

As repressed sadists are supposed to become policemen or butchers, so those with irrational fear of life become publishers.
Cyril Connolly

♋

No news is good news; no journalism is even better.
Nicholas Bentley, artist and journalist (1907-1978)

Journalism largely consists in saying 'Lord Jones Dead' to people who never knew Lord Jones was alive.
G. K. Chesterton

If you can't annoy somebody, there's little point in writing.
Kingsley Amis, novelist (1922-1995)

A good novel tells us the truth about its hero; but a bad novel tells us the truth about its author.
G. K. Chesterton

Television thrives on unreason, and unreason thrives on television. It strikes at the emotions rather than the intellect.
Robin Day, political interviewer (1923-2000)

♋

The world may be full of fourth-rate writers but it's also full of fourth-rate readers.
Stan Barstow, novelist and playwright

♋

The quarrels of popes and kings, with wars and pestilences in every page; the men all so good for nothing, and hardly any women at all – it is very tiresome.
Jane Austen, writer (1775-1817) on history

The pen is mightier than the sword, and considerably easier to write with.
Marty Feldman

♋

By increasing the size of the keyhole, today's playwrights are in danger of doing away with the door.
Peter Ustinov

♋

Somerset Maugham said there were three rules for writing – and nobody knows what they are.
Joan Collins, actress

By office boys for office boys.
Lord Salisbury, politician on *Daily Mail*

☞

I don't see why people are so snooty about Channel 5. It has some respectable documentaries about the Second World War. It also devotes considerable airtime to investigations into lapdancing, and other related and vital subjects.
Boris Johnson

☞

Definition of a classic: a book everyone is assumed to have read and often thinks they have.
Alan Bennett

He likes publicity. He wears a card round his neck saying, 'In case of heart attack, call a press conference'.
Tommy Docherty on Manchester City chairman Peter Swales

℅

You will, I am sure, agree with me that... if page 534 only finds us in the second chapter, the length of the first one must have been really intolerable.
Arthur Conan Doyle, writer (1859-1930)

℅

Playwrights are like men who have been dining for a month in an Indian restaurant. After eating curry night after night, they deny the existence of asparagus.
Peter Ustinov

They are so filthy and bestial that no honest man would admit one into his house for a water-closet doormat.
Charles Dickens on newspapers

ॐ

I don't watch television, I think it destroys the art of talking about oneself.
Stephen Fry, comedian and actor

ॐ

The tabloids are like animals, with their own behavioural patterns. There's no point in complaining about them, any more than complaining that lions might eat you.
David Mellor, politician

I know I was writing stories when I was five. I don't know what I did before that. Just loafed I suppose.
P. G. Wodehouse

ॐ

Particularly against books the Home Secretary is. If we can't stamp out literature in the country, we can at least stop it being brought in from outside.
Evelyn Waugh

ॐ

I have only read one book in my life and that is *White Fang*. It's so frightfully good I've never bothered to read another.
Nancy Mitford

Almost anyone can be an author; the business is to collect money and fame from that state of being.
A. A. Milne, writer (1882-1956)

I can't understand these chaps who go round American universities explaining how they write poems: It's like going round explaining how you sleep with your wife.
Philip Larkin, poet (1922-1985)

# England and the English

You are offered a piece of bread and butter that feels like a damp handkerchief and sometimes, when cucumber is added to it, like a wet one.
Sir Compton Mackenzie, novelist and politician (1883-1972) on an English tea party

♋

But Lord! to see the absurd nature of Englishmen, that cannot forbear laughing and jeering at everything that looks strange.
Samuel Pepys, writer (1633-1703)

♋

We [the English] seem, as it were, to have conquered and peopled half the world in a fit of absence of mind.
John Seeley, politician (1834-1895)

That knuckle-end of England – that land of Calvin, oat-cakes, and sulphur.
Revd Sydney Smith

What two ideas are more inseparable than Beer and Britannia?
Revd Sydney Smith

What a pity it is that we have no amusements in England but vice and religion!
Revd Sydney Smith

# England and the English

The English instinctively admire any man with no talent and is modest about it.
James Agate, critic (1877-1947)

♋

We English are good at forgiving our enemies; it releases us from the obligation of liking our friends.
P. D. James

♋

The Welsh are so damn Welsh that it looks like affectation.
Alexander Raleigh, poet (1534-1618) to D. B. Wyndham Lewis

The noblest prospect which a Scotchman ever sees is the high-road that leads him to England.
Samuel Johnson

᧯

This island is made mainly of coal and surrounded by fish. Only an organising genius could produce a shortage of coal and fish at the same time.
Aneurin Bevan

᧯

Dialect words – those terrible marks of the beast to the truly genteel.
Thomas Hardy

It's a ghastly place. Huge gangs of tough sinewy men roam the valleys terrorising people with their close-harmony singing. You need half a pint of phlegm in your throat just to pronounce the placenames. Never ask for directions in Wales Baldrick, you'll be washing spit out of your hair for a fortnight.
Rowan Atkinson on Wales, *Blackadder*

♋

He muffs his real job without a blush, and yet he would rather be shot than do his bootlaces up criss-cross.
H. G. Wells on the British Officer

♋

I have been trying all my life to like Scotchmen, and am obliged to desist from the experiment in despair.
Charles Lamb

The British electors will not vote for a man who doesn't wear a hat.
Lord Beaverbrook, newspaper magnate (1879-1964), advice to Lord Driberg

You have to give this much to the Luftwaffe - when it knocked down our buildings it didn't replace them with anything more offensive than rubble. We did that.
Prince Charles

Bugger Bognor!
King George V

There are still parts of Wales where the only concession to gaiety is a striped shroud.
Gwyn Thomas, writer and dramatist (1913-1981)

♋

The English Winter – ending in July
to recommence in August.
Lord Byron

♋

I like the English. They have the most rigid code of immorality in the world.
Malcolm Bradbury, novelist

The English never draw a line without blurring it.
Winston Churchill

✆

When two Englishmen meet, their first talk is of the weather.
Samuel Johnson

✆

Britain is too small; if you have a high powered car to drive around in it's like a roundabout.
Will Self

On a global scale British mountains are pathetic, Snowdon and Ben Nevis being roughly the same height as the speed humps they install on Swiss roads to slow down traffic.
Hugh Dennis, comedian

♋

Kent, sir – everybody knows Kent – apples, cherries, hops, and women.
Charles Dickens, *The Pickwick Papers*, (1836-1837)

♋

The British do not expect happiness. I had the impression, all the time that I lived there, that they do not want to be happy; they want to be right.
Quentin Crisp

How amazing that the language of a few thousand savages living on a fog-encrusted island in the North Sea should become the language of the world.

Norman St John-Stevas, politician

# Countryside and the City

It is my belief, Watson, founded upon my experience, that the lowest and vilest alleys of London do not present a more dreadful record of sin than does the smiling and beautiful countryside.

Arthur Conan Doyle, *The Adventures of Sherlock Holmes*, *The Copper Beeches*, (1892)

Anybody can be good in the country. There are no temptations there.

Oscar Wilde, *The Picture of Dorian Gray*

Clearly, then, the city is not a concrete jungle,
it is a human zoo.
Desmond Morris, scientist, *The Human Zoo*, 1969

I have no relish for the country; it is a kind of
healthy grave.
Revd Sydney Smith

It is a place with only one post a day... In the
country I always fear that creation will expire
before tea-time.
Revd Sydney Smith

If you would be known, and not know, vegetate in a village; if you would know, and not be known, live in a city.
Charles Caleb Colton, writer (1780-1832)

၆

When I am in the country I wish to vegetate like the country.
William Hazlitt, critic (1778-1830) *On Going a Journey*, 1822

၆

London, that great cesspool into which all the loungers of the Empire are irresistibly drained.
Arthur Conan Doyle, *A Study in Scarlet*, 1887

I have never understood why anybody agreed to go on being a rustic after about 1400.
Kingsley Amis, *The Green Man*, 1969

My living in Yorkshire was so far out of the way, that it was actually twelve miles from a lemon.
Revd Sydney Smith

I don't like the provinces. You can't eat and you can't get clean shirts.
Mick Jagger, musician

God made the country, and man made the town.
William Cowper, poet (1731-1800)

∽

No city should be too large for a man to walk out of in a morning.
Cyril Connolly

∽

I've made an odd discovery. Every time I talk to a savant I feel quite sure that happiness is no longer a possibility. Yet when I talk with my gardener, I'm convinced of the opposite.
Bertrand Russell

London! the needy villain's general home,
The common sewer of Paris and of Rome!
With eager thirst, by folly or by fate,
Sucks in the dregs of each corrupted state.
Samuel Johnson, *London*, 1738

♋

In my time, the follies of the town crept slowly among us, but now they travel faster than a stage-coach.
Oliver Goldsmith

♋

I nauseate walking; 'tis a country diversion, I loathe the country.
William Congreve, *The Way of the World*

God the first garden made, and the first city
Cain.
Abraham Cowley, poet (1616-1667)

♋

A small country town is not the place in which
one would choose to quarrel with a wife; every
human being in such places is a spy.
Samuel Johnson

♋

Poverty, to be picturesque, should be rural.
Suburban misery is as hideous as it is pitiable.
Anthony Trollope, author (1815-1882)

Dear, damned, distracting town.
Alexander Pope on London

♋

Hell is a city much like London –
A populous and a smoky city;
There are all sorts of people undone,
And there is little or no fun done;
Small justice shown, and still less pity.
Percy Bysshe Shelley, poet (1792-1822)

♋

For Cambridge people rarely smile,
Being urban, squat, and packed with guile.
Rupert Brooke, poet (1887-1915)

♋

The great thing about Glasgow is that if there's
a nuclear attack it'll look exactly the same
afterwards.
Billy Connolly

# Old Age

To get back my youth I would do anything in the world, except take exercise, get up early, or be respectable.
Oscar Wilde, *The Picture of Dorian Gray*, 1891

♋

The older one grows, the more one likes indecency.
Virginia Woolf

♋

The greatest problem about old age is the fear that it may go on too long.
A. J. P. Taylor, historian (1906-1990) quoted in *The Observer*

Growing old is like being increasingly penalised for a crime you haven't committed.
Anthony Powell, novelist, *A Dance to the Music of Time: Temporary Kings*, 1951-1975

♋

I refuse to admit that I am more than 52, even if that makes my children illegitimate.
Nancy Astor

♋

Pushing forty? She's hanging on for dear life.
Ivy Compton-Burnett

At 50, everyone has the face he deserves.
George Orwell

♋

There is only one cure for grey hair. It was invented by a Frenchman. It is called the guillotine.
P. G. Wodehouse

♋

Old age, believe me, is a good and pleasant thing. It is true you are gently shouldered off the stage, but then you are given such a comfortable front stall as spectator.
Jane Harrison, writer (1850-1928)

Time and trouble will tame an advanced young woman, but an advanced old woman is uncontrollable by any earthly force.
Dorothy L. Sayers

❧

Regrets are the natural property of grey hairs.
Charles Dickens

❧

The years between 50 and 70 are the hardest. You are always asked to do things, and yet you are not decrepit enough to turn them down.
T. S. Eliot

# Old Age

Middle age is youth without levity, and age without decay.
Daniel Defoe, wtiter (1660-1731)

♋

A man explained inflation to his wife thus: 'When we married, you measured 36-24-36. Now you're 42-42-42. There's more of you, but you are not worth as much.'
Lord Barnett, Labour peer

♋

The past is the only dead thing that smells sweet.
Cyril Connolly

When you're my age you never risk being ill –
because everyone says: oh, he's done for.
John Gielgud, actor (1904-2000)

♋

An archaeologist is the best husband a woman
can have: the older she gets, the more
interested he is in her.
Agatha Christie

♋

I have the body of an eighteen year old. I keep
it in the fridge.
Spike Milligan

# Old Age

One of the many pleasures of old age is giving things up.
Malcolm Muggeridge, broadcaster (1903-1990)

☞

Well, I suppose I must attribute it to the fact that I haven't died yet.
Malcolm Sargent, conductor (1895-1967) on being asked to what he attributed his advanced age of 70

☞

You will recognize, my boy, the first sign of old age: it is when you go out into the streets of London and realise for the first time how young the policemen look.
Edward Seymour Hicks, actor and dramatic author (1871-1949)

Memorial services are the cocktail parties of the geriatric set.
Harold Macmillan

ॐ

He that loves a rosy cheek
Or a coral lip admires
Or, from star-like eyes, doth seek
Fuel to maintain his fires;
As old Time makes these decay
So his flames must waste away.
Thomas Carew (c.1595-1639), *Disdain Returned*

ॐ

I want to be young and wild, and then I want to be middle-aged and rich, and then I want to be old and annoy people by pretending I'm deaf.
Rowan Atkinson, *Blackadder*

# Old Age

We are happier in many ways when we are old than when we are young. The young sow wild oats, the old grow sage.
Winston Churchill

♋

Though I be hoor, I fare as dooth a tree
That blosmeth er that fruyt ywoxen bee;
And blosmy tree nys neither drye ne deed.
I feele me nowhere hoor but on myn heed.
Geoffrey Chaucer, *The Merchant's Tale*

♋

I can still rock like a son of a bitch.
Ozzy Osbourne, musician

♋

The long dull monotonous years of middle-aged prosperity or middle-aged adversity are excellent campaigning weather for the Devil.
C. S. Lewis

# Science and Technology

Multimedia? As far as I'm concerned, it's reading with the radio on!
Rory Bremner, comedian

℅

I think animal testing is a terrible thing. They get all nervous and give silly answers.
Stephen Fry

℅

Reading computer manuals without the hardware is as frustrating as reading sex manuals without the software.
Arthur C. Clarke

Science in the modern world has many uses;
its chief use, however, is to provide long words
to cover the errors of the rich.
G. K. Chesterton, *Heretics*, 1905

♋

Television is more interesting than people. If
it were not, we should have people standing
in the corners of our rooms.
Alan Coren, writer, *The Times*

♋

I have had my television aerials removed. It's
the moral equivalent of a prostate operation.
Malcolm Muggeridge

In science the credit goes to the man who convinces the world, not to the man to whom the idea first occurs.
Francis Darwin, botanist (1848-1925)

∞

Any sufficiently advanced technology is indistinguishable from magic.
Arthur C. Clarke

∞

Ignorance more frequently begets confidence than does knowledge: it is those who know little, not those who know much, who so positively assert that this or that problem will never be solved by science.
Charles Darwin, scientist (1809-1882)

Television is like the invention of indoor plumbing. It didn't change people's habits. It just kept them inside the house.
Alfred Hitchcock

☞

Personally, I don't think there's intelligent life on other planets. Why should other planets be any different from this one?
Bob Monkhouse

☞

If the world should blow itself up, the last audible voice would be that of an expert saying it can't be done.
Peter Ustinov

Everything starts somewhere, although many physicists disagree.
Terry Pratchett

Technological progress has merely provided us with more efficient means for going backwards.
Aldous Huxley

The greatest task before civilisation at present is to make machines what they ought to be, the slaves, instead of the masters of men.
Havelock Ellis

I've got the film rights of *Waiting for Godot* from Samuel Beckett. He said it was impossible. Then, I told him about the talkies. The last film he saw was Buster Keaton.

Peter O'Toole, actor

☉

I am amazed at radio DJ's today. I am firmly convinced that AM on my radio stands for Absolute Moron. I will not begin to tell you what FM stands for.

Jasper Carrott, comedian

☉

A common mistake that people make when trying to design something completely foolproof is to underestimate the ingenuity of complete fools.

Douglas Adams

Invention, it must be humbly admitted, does not consist of creating out of void, but out of chaos.

Mary Shelley, author (1797-1851)

෨

Space isn't remote at all. It's only an hour's drive away if your car could go straight upwards.

Fred Hoyle, scientist (1915-2001)

෨

The earth's crust is basically a jerry-built botch of a job that no structural surveyor would pass if you applied for a mortgage on it.

Hugh Dennis

I don't think necessity is the mother of invention – invention, in my opinion, arises directly from idleness, possibly also from laziness. To save oneself trouble.
Agatha Christie

The e-mail of the species is more deadly than the mail.
Stephen Fry

Technology… is a queer thing. It brings you great gifts with one hand, and it stabs you in the back with the other.
C. P. Snow, author and physicist (1905-1980)

The man who invented the zip fastener was today honoured with a lifetime peerage. He'll now be known as the Lord of the Flies.
Ronnie Barker, actor and writer

# Youth and Education

Youth is a wonderful thing. What a crime to waste it on children.
George Bernard Shaw

♋

I don't dislike babies, though I think very young ones rather disgusting.
Queen Victoria

♋

An ugly baby is a very nasty object, and the prettiest is frightful when undressed.
Queen Victoria

Young men think old men are fools; but old men know young men are fools.
George Chapman, poet (1559-1634)

∞

What is youth except a man or a woman before it is ready or fit to be seen?
Evelyn Waugh

∞

There is no sinner like a young saint.
Aphra Behn, dramatist (1640-1689)

It is no wonder that people are so horrible
when they start their life as children.
Kingsley Amis

♋

As a child, I thought I hated everybody, but
when I grew up I realised it was just children I
didn't like.
Philip Larkin

♋

I think we can rely on time to remedy that,
sire.
William Pitt the Younger, former Prime Minister (1759-1806)
on being faced by George III's surprise at his young age

I was a modest, good-humoured boy. It is Oxford that has made me insufferable.
Max Beerbohm

♋

Youth is wholly experimental.
Robert Louis Stevenson

♋

On every formal visit a child ought to be of the party by way of provision for discourse.
Jane Austen

Teach him to think for himself? Oh my God, teach him rather to think like other people.
Mary Shelley on her son's education

I would there were no age between sixteen and three-and-twenty, or that youth would sleep out the rest; for there is nothing in the between but getting wenches with child, wronging the ancientry, stealing, fighting.
William Shakespeare, *The Winter's Tale*

Universities incline wits to sophistry and affectation.
Francis Bacon

Be on the alert to recognise your prime at whatever time of your life it may occur.
Muriel Spark

♋

Getting an education was a bit like a communicable sexual disease. It made you unsuitable for a lot of jobs and then you had the urge to pass it on.
Terry Pratchett

♋

University degrees are a bit like adultery: you may not want to get involved in that sort of thing, but you don't want to be thought incapable.
Peter Imbert, Commissioner of the Metropolitan Police

I am fond of children – except boys.
Lewis Carroll, writer (1832-1898)

♋

Children with Hyacinth's temperament don't know better as they grow older; they merely know more.
Saki

♋

Age may have one side, but assuredly Youth has the other. There is nothing more certain than that both are right, except perhaps that both are wrong.
Robert Burns

Intense, moody, incredible charisma. Short, myopic, not good-looking. You know who he was like? A young Woody Allen.
Joan Collins on James Dean

၆

When you've seen a nude infant doing a backward somersault you know why clothing exists.
Stephen Fry

၆

The future we're leaving our children is less an ecological legacy, more a pre-emptive strike.
Rob Newman, comedian and author

# Youth and Education

The intelligence of the planet is constant and the population is growing.
Arthur C. Clarke

☞

The dons of Oxford and Cambridge are too busy educating the young men to be able to teach them anything.
Samuel Butler

☞

Young women especially have something invested in being nice people, and it's only when you have children that you realise you're not a nice person at all, but generally a selfish bully.
Fay Weldon, novelist

Thank goodness I was never sent to school; it would have rubbed off some of the originality.
Beatrix Potter, author (1866-1943)

Education is the period during which you are being instructed by somebody you do not know, about something you do not want to know.
G. K. Chesterton

# Eating and Drinking

A woman should never be seen eating or drinking, unless it be lobster salad and Champagne, the only true feminine and becoming viands.
Lord Byron

The secret of a successful restaurant is sharp knives.
George Orwell

If I had been around when Rubens was painting, I would have been revered as a fabulous model. Kate Moss? Well, she would have been the paintbrush.
Dawn French, comedienne and actress

Who discovered we could get milk from cows, and what did he THINK he was doing at the time?
Billy Connolly

Chopsticks are one of the reasons the Chinese never invented custard.
Spike Milligan

Vegetarianism is harmless enough, though it is apt to fill a man with wind and self-righteousness.
Robert Hutchinson, doctor (1871-1960)

೨

Music with dinner is an insult both to the cook and the violinist.
G. K. Chesterton

೨

A social conscience is like a garden fence, you try to eat it, it'll get stuck in your throat.
Mike from *The Young Ones*

Some day you'll eat a pork chop, Joey, and then
God help all women.
Mrs. Patrick Campbell, actress (1865-1940) to George Bernard
Shaw, a vegetarian

♋

Good apple pies are a considerable part of our
domestic happiness.
Jane Austen

♋

I am a great eater of beef, and I believe that
does harm to my wit.
William Shakespeare, *Twelfth Night*

Heaven sends us good meat, but the Devil sends cooks.
David Garrick, actor and playwright (1717-1779)

♋

The best number for a dinner party is two – myself and a damn good head waiter.
Nubar Gulbenkian, philanthropist (1896-1972)

♋

All happiness depends on a leisurely breakfast.
John Gunther, journalist (1901-1970)

Words are the leaves; and where they most abound, much fruit of sense beneath is rarely found.
Alexander Pope

ॐ

The salmon are striking back.
The Queen Mother (1900-2002) when choking on a fish bone

ॐ

Life's too short to stuff a mushroom.
Shirley Conran, author

# Eating and Drinking

I tell you one thing. I've been to a parallel universe, I've seen time running backwards, I've played pool with planets, and I've given birth to twins, but I never thought in my entire life I'd taste an edible Pot Noodle.
Lister, *Red Dwarf*

If more of us valued food and cheer and song above hoarded gold, it would be a merrier world.
J. R. R. Tolkien, writer (1892-1973)

How good one feels when one is full – how satisfied with ourselves and with the world! People who have tried it, tell me that a clear conscience makes you very happy and contented; but a full stomach does the business quite as well, and is cheaper, and more easily obtained. One feels so forgiving and generous after a substantial and well-digested meal – so noble-minded, so kindly-hearted.
Jerome K. Jerome, *Three Men in a Boat*, 1979

♋

There are two types of women in this world, those who like chocolate and complete bitches.
Dawn French

♋

I'm already two years ahead on my daily fat allowance. I'm looking for skinny people to see if I can borrow theirs.
Jo Brand, comedienne

## Eating and Drinking

I also attempted a personal challenge to eat my bodyweight in Belgian chocolate. After the first couple of kilos in the art gallery, the Magritte pictures appeared to be moving. After a few more, in a chocolate haze, I heard the voice of Tin Tin telling me to kill the Smurfs.
Ross Noble, comedian, interview with chortle.co.uk

If slaughterhouses had glass walls, everyone would be a vegetarian.
Paul McCartney, musician

The proof that God has a very weird sense of humour is that, having invented the sublime mystery of haute cuisine, he went and gave it to the French.
A. A. Gill

My advice if you insist on slimming: eat as much as you like – just don't swallow it.
Harry Secombe, actor (1921-2001)

Poets have been mysteriously silent on the subject of cheese.
G. K. Chesterton

Enclosing every thin man, there's a fat man demanding elbow-room.
Evelyn Waugh

# Eating and Drinking

I have taken more good from alcohol than alcohol has taken from me.
Winston Churchill

♋

My rule of life prescribed as an absolutely sacred rite smoking cigars and also the drinking of alcohol before, after, and if need be during all meals and in the intervals between them.
Winston Churchill

♋

Alcohol is the anesthesia by which we endure the operation of life.
George Bernard Shaw

If you resolve to give up smoking, drinking and loving, you don't actually live longer; it just seems longer.
Clement Freud, politician

☞

The people who are regarded as moral luminaries are those who forego ordinary pleasures and find compensation in interfering with the pleasures of others.
Bertrand Russell, *Sceptical Essays*, 1928

☞

No animal ever invented anything so bad as drunkenness – or so good as drink.
G. K. Chesterton

# Eating and Drinking

Claret is the liquor for boys; port for men; but he who aspires to be a hero... must drink brandy.
A. E. Housman, poet (1859-1936)

♋

I'm only a beer teetotaller, not a champagne teetotaller. I don't like beer.
George Bernard Shaw

♋

In 1969 I gave up drinking and sex. It was the worst 20 minutes of my life.
George Best

A man who exposes himself when he is intoxicated, has not the art of getting drunk.
Samuel Johnson

☙

'Tis not the drinking that is to be blamed, but the excess.
John Selden, statesman (1584-1654)

☙

O God, that men should put an enemy in their mouths to steal away their brains! That we should with joy, pleasance, revel, and applause transform ourselves into beasts!
William Shakespeare, *Othello*

It provokes the desire but it takes away the performance. Therefore much drink may be said to be an equivocator with lechery: it makes him and it mars him; it sets him on and it takes him off.
William Shakespeare, *Macbeth*

♋

A tavern is a place where madness is sold by the bottle.
Jonathan Swift, writer (1667-1745)

♋

If the headache would only precede the intoxication, alcoholism would be a virtue.
Samuel Butler

My favourite drink is a cocktail of carrot juice and whisky. I am always drunk but I can see for miles.
Roy Brown

♋

Gentlemen who use MSS as drunkards use lamp-posts – not to light them on their way but to dissimulate their instability.
A. E. Housman

♋

Coffee in England always tastes like a chemistry experiment.
Agatha Christie

I like my coffee like I like my women. In a plastic cup.
Eddie Izzard

ॐ

Never drink black coffee at lunch; it will keep you awake all afternoon.
Jilly Cooper, writer

ॐ

And Noah he often said to his wife when they sat down to dine,
 'I don't care where the water goes if it doesn't go into the wine'.
G. K. Chesterton

Hotel tea is when you have to mix together a plastic envelope containing too much sugar, a small plastic pot of something which is not milk but has curdled anyway, and a thin brown packet seemingly containing the ashes of a cremated mole.

Frank Muir, author and comedian (1920-1998)

###

Many, being reasonable, must get drunk;
The best of life is but intoxication.

Lord Byron

###

There's nothing worse than an introspective drunk.

Tom Sharpe, comic, novelist and historian

I've stopped drinking, but only while I'm asleep.
George Best

Bacchus hath drowned more men than Neptune.
Thomas Fuller, clergyman (1608-1661)

Ale, man, ale's the stuff to drink
For fellows whom it hurts to think.
A. E. Housman

If you drink it straight down, you can feel it going into each individual intestine.
Richard Burton

Eating and Drinking

185

# Love, Marriage and Sex

Men always want to be a woman's first love –
women like to be a man's last romance.
Oscar Wilde, *A Woman of No Importance*

♋

Frailty, thy name is woman!
William Shakespeare, *Hamlet*

♋

That man that hath a tongue, I say, is no man,
If with his tongue he cannot win a woman.
William Shakespeare, *The Two Gentlemen of Verona*

As blushing will sometimes make a whore pass
for a virtuous woman, so modesty may make
a fool seem a man of sense.
Jonathan Swift

෨

When a woman marries again, it is because she
detested her first husband. When a man
marries again, it is because he adored his first
wife. Women try their luck; men risk theirs.
Oscar Wilde, *The Picture of Dorian Gray*

෨

Men at most differ as Heaven and Earth, but
women, worst and best, as Heaven and Hell.
Alfred Lord Tennyson, poet (1809-1892)

A man… is *so* in the way in the house!
Mrs Gaskell

She's the sort of woman who lives for others and you can tell the others by their hunted expression.
C. S. Lewis

Men are people, just like women.
Fenella Fielding, actress

If I were a girl, I'd despair. The supply of good women far exceeds that of the men who deserve them.
Robert Graves

🦀

Being powerful is like being a lady. If you have to tell people you are, you aren't.
Margaret Thatcher

🦀

The first time Adam had the chance, he put the blame on a woman.
Nancy Astor

You see, dear, it is not true that woman was made from man's rib; she was really made from his funny bone.
James M. Barrie

ॐ

In the sex war, thoughtlessness is the weapon of the male, vindictiveness of the female.
Cyril Connolly

ॐ

Men have charisma; women have vital statistics.
Julie Birchill, writer

A woman is only a woman, but a good cigar is a smoke.
Rudyard Kipling

♋

The claim to equality is made only by those who feel themselves to be in some way inferior.
C. S. Lewis

♋

It goes far towards reconciling me to being a woman when I reflect I am thus in no danger of marrying one.
Lady Wortley Montagu, writer (1689-1762)

We are not asking for superiority for we have always had that; all we ask is equality.
Nancy Astor

♋

No nice men are good at getting taxis.
Katherine Whitehorn, journalist

♋

Women should have labels on their foreheads saying, 'Government Health Warning: women can seriously damage your brains, genitals, current account, confidence, razor blades, and good standing among your friends'.
Jeffrey Bernard

# Love, Marriage and Sex

A woman's always younger than a man of equal years.
Elizabeth Barrett Browning, poet (1806-1861)

♋

It will all go on as long as women are stupid enough to go on bringing men into the world.
Dorothy Miller Richardson, novelist (1873-1957)

♋

Marriage is a wonderful invention. But, then again, so is the bicycle repair kit.
Billy Connolly

Maids want nothing but husbands, and when they have them, they want everything.
William Shakespeare

Remember if you marry for beauty, thou bindest thyself all thy life for that which perchance, will neither last nor please thee one year: and when thou hast it, it will be to thee of no price at all.
Walter Raleigh, courtier, explorer, historian (1552-1618)

I haven't spoken to my wife for over a month. We haven't had a row – it's just that I'm afraid to interrupt her.
Les Dawson, comedian (1934-1993)

# Love, Marriage and Sex

I once placed an ad in the personal columns of *Private Eye* saying that I wanted to meet a rich well-insured widow with a view to murdering her.  I got 48 replies.
Spike Milligan

♋

We were happily married for eight months. Unfortunately, we were married for four and a half years.
Nick Faldo, golfer

♋

I married beneath me – all women do.
Nancy Astor

I feel sure that no girl would go to the altar if she knew all.
Queen Victoria

Ꮟ

Though women are angels, yet wedlock's the devil!
Lord Byron, *To Eliza*

Ꮟ

I have met with women whom I really think would like to be married to a poem, and to be given away by a novel.
John Keats, poet (1795-1821) to Fanny Brawne

Strange to say what delight we married people have to see these poor fools decoyed into our condition.
Samuel Pepys

⌘

Advice to persons about to marry – 'Don't.'
Henry Mayhew, writer (1812-1887)

⌘

My definition of marriage… it resembles a pair of shears, so joined that they cannot be separated; often moving in opposite directions, yet always punishing anyone who comes between them.
Revd Sydney Smith

Instead of getting married again, I'm going to find a woman I don't like and just give her a house.
Rod Stewart, musician

Laugh and the world laughs with you. Snore and you sleep alone.
Anthony Burgess

A sort of friendship recognised by the police.
Robert Louis Stevenson on marriage

Perfection is what American women expect to find in their husbands... but English women only hope to find in their butlers.
W. Somerset Maugham

♋

My wife and I were married in a toilet: it was a marriage of convenience.
Tommy Cooper

♋

Marriage is the result of the longing for the deep, deep peace of the double bed after the hurly-burly of the chaise-longue.
Mrs. Patrick Campbell

A lady's imagination is very rapid; it jumps from admiration to love, from love to matrimony in a moment.

Jane Austen

♋

His designs were strictly honourable, as the phrase is; that is, to rob a lady of her fortune by way of marriage.

Henry Fielding, novelist (1707-1754) *Tom Jones*, 1749

♋

Here lies my wife. Here let her lie! Now she's at rest, And so am I.

John Dryden, poet (1631-1700), a proposed epitaph for his wife

It was very good of God to let Carlyle and Mrs Carlyle marry one another and so make only two people miserable instead of four.
Samuel Johnson on Thomas Carlyle and his wife

♋

The dread of loneliness is greater than the fear of bondage, so we get married.
Cyril Connolly

♋

Marriage is at best a dangerous experiment.
Thomas Love Peacock, author (1785-1866)

Marriage is the waste-paper basket of the emotions.
Sidney Webb, writer (1859-1947)

♋

A bachelor lives like a king and dies like a beggar.
L. S. Lowry, painter (1887-1976)

♋

When a man opens the car door for his wife, it's either a new car or a new wife.
Prince Philip, Duke of Edinburgh

It destroys one's nerves to be amiable everyday to the same human being.
Benjamin Disraeli

♋

The world must be peopled. When I said I would die a bachelor, I did not think I should live till I were married.
William Shakespeare, *Much Ado About Nothing*

♋

Many a good hanging prevents a bad marriage.
William Shakespeare, *Twelfth Night*

Courtship to marriage, as a very witty prologue to a very dull play.
William Congreve, *The Old Bachelor*

♋

She was a worthy womman al hir lyve
Housbondes at chirche-dore she hadde fyve
Withouten other companye in youthe.
Geoffrey Chaucer, *The Canterbury Tales*

♋

We invite people like that to tea, but we don't marry them.
Lady Chetwode on her future son-in-law John Betjeman

## Love, Marriage and Sex

Love's like the measles – all the worse when it comes late in life.
Douglas Jerrold

🦀

My mental hands were empty, and I felt I must do something as a counterirritant or antibody to my hysterical alarm at getting married at the age of 43.
Ian Fleming

🦀

Music makes one feel so romantic – at least it always gets on one's nerves – which is the same thing nowadays.
Oscar Wilde, *A Woman of No Importance*

It is a curious thought, but it is only when you see people looking ridiculous that you realise just how much you love them.
Agatha Christie

♋

Love is like the measles; we all have to go through it.
Jerome K. Jerome

♋

Love is a device invented by bank managers to make us overdrawn.
Rimmer, *Red Dwarf*

# Love, Marriage and Sex

If music be the food of love, let's have a Beethoven butty.
John Lennon, musician (1940-80)

☋

People in love, it is well known, suffer extreme conceptual delusions; the most common of these being that other people find your condition as thrilling and eye-watering as you do yourselves.
Julian Barnes, writer in *The Observer*

☋

To fall in love you have to be in the state of mind for it to take, like a disease.
Nancy Mitford

When people say, 'You're breaking my heart,' they do in fact usually mean that you're breaking their genitals.
Jeffrey Bernard

♋

Nothing is to be done without a bribe I find, in love as well as law.
Susannah Centlivre, dramatist and actress (c.1667-1723)

♋

The lunatic, the lover and the poet
Are of imagination all compact.
William Shakespeare, *A Midsummer Night's Dream*

Friendship is a disinterested commerce between equals; love, an abject intercourse between tyrants and slaves.
Oliver Goldsmith

ॐ

Friendship often ends in love; but love in friendship – never.
Charles Caleb Colton

ॐ

One should always be in love. That is the reason one should never marry.
Oscar Wilde, *A Woman of No Importance*

Thrice happy's the wooing that's not long adoing. So much time is saved in the billing and cooing.

Richard Harris Barham, writer (1788-1845), *Sir Rupert the Fearless*

♋

'Yes,' I answered you last night;
'No,' this morning, sir, I say:
Colours seen by candle-light
Will not look the same by day.

Elizabeth Barrett Browning, *The Lady's "Yes"*, (1844)

♋

The surest way to hit a woman's heart is to take aim kneeling.

Douglas Jerrold

They dream in courtship, but in wedlock
wake.
Alexander Pope

♋

Any woman can fool a man if she wants to
and if he's in love with her.
Agatha Christie

♋

Love may not make the world go round, but I
must admit that it makes the ride worthwhile.
Sean Connery

I'm afraid I was very much the traditionalist. I went down on one knee and dictated a proposal which my secretary faxed over straight away.
Stephen Fry

♋

Marriage is an adventure, like going to war.
G. K. Chesteron

♋

[Dancing is] a perpendicular expression of a horizontal desire.
George Bernard Shaw in *The Statesman*

The only good thing about the Spice Girls is that you can look at them with the sound turned down.
George Harrison, musician (19743-2001) in *Rolling Stone* re: Mouthing Off

♋

Marriage has many pains but celibacy has no pleasures.
Samuel Johnson, *Rasselas* (1759)

♋

The important thing in acting is to be able to laugh and cry. If I have to cry, I think of my sex life. If I have to laugh, I think of my sex life.
Glenda Jackson

The expense is damnable, the position is ridiculous, and the pleasure fleeting.
Samuel Johnson

♋

The way to tell if a man is sexually excited is if he's breathing.
Jo Brand

♋

Outside every thin girl is a fat man, trying to get in.
Katherine Whitehorn

I think I mentioned to Bob [Geldof] I could make love for eight hours. What I didn't say was that this included four hours of begging and then dinner and a movie.
Sting, musician

♋

Love and scandal are the best sweeteners of tea.
Henry Fielding

♋

Your old virginity is like one of our French withered pears: it looks ill, it eats dryly.
William Shakespeare, *All's Well that Ends Well*

Girls are like pianos. When they're not upright, they're grand.
Benny Hill

♋

For a long time, I thought coq au vin meant love in a lorry.
Victoria Wood

♋

I don't mind where people make love, so long as they don't do it in the street and frighten the horses.
Mrs. Patrick Campbell

# Love, Marriage and Sex

Female dinner guest: Mr. Churchill, I care neither for your politics nor your moustache

Churchill: Do not distress yourself, you are very unlikely to come into contact with either

♋

If our sex life were determined by our first youthful experiments, most of the world would be doomed to celibacy. In no area of human experience are human beings more convinced that something better can be had if only they persevere.
P. D. James

♋

I think people should be free to engage in any sexual practices they choose; they should draw the line at goats though.
Elton John, musician

My wife is a sex object. Every time I ask for
sex, she objects.
Les Dawson

☞

I became one of the stately homos of England.
Quentin Crisp

☞

I don't fancy models as much as I should. The
older I get, the more I like meat with my gravy.
Hugh Grant, actor

Men get laid, but women get screwed.
Quentin Crisp

♋

I can still enjoy sex at 74 – I live at 75 so it's no distance.
Bob Monkhouse

♋

His mouth is a no-go area. It's like kissing the Berlin Wall.
Helena Bonham Carter, actress, on kissing Woody Allen

I'm not against half-naked girls – not as often as I'd like to be...
Benny Hill

❧

It's not important to me. It would be important if I wasn't getting any.
Michael Caine

❧

Masturbation is always very safe. You not only control the person you're with but you can leave when you want to.
Dudley Moore

An intellectual is a person who's found one thing that's more interesting than sex.
Aldous Huxley

♋

Sex: the pleasure is momentary, the position ridiculous, and the expense damnable.
Lord Chesterfield

♋

The tragedy is when you've got sex in the head instead of down where it belongs.
D. H. Lawrence, writer (1885-1930)

Its avowed purpose is to excite sexual desire, which, I should have thought, is unnecessary in the case of the young, inconvenient in the case of the middle aged, and unseemly in the old.
Malcolm Muggeridge on pornography

My message to the businessman of this country when they go abroad on business is that there is one thing above all they can take with them to stop them catching AIDS, and that is the wife.
Edwina Curry, former Junior Health Minister

Show me a man who loves football and nine times out of ten you'll be pointing at a really bad shag.
Julie Birchill

There comes a moment in the day when you have written your pages in the morning, attended to your correspondence in the afternoon, and have nothing further to do. Then comes that hour when you are bored; that's the time for sex.
H. G. Wells

Sex is the mysticism of materialism and the only possible religion in a materialistic society.
Malcolm Muggeridge

Sex – the great inequality, the great miscalculator, the great irritator.
Enid Bagnold, novelist (1889-1981)

# Families and Friends

A family is a tyranny ruled over by its weakest member.
George Bernard Shaw

The excessive regard of parents for their children, and their dislike of other people's is, like class feeling, patriotism, save-your-soul-ism, and other virtues, a mean exclusiveness at bottom.
Thomas Hardy

The trouble with children is that they are not returnable.
Quentin Crisp

# Families and Friends

We make our friends; we make our enemies;
but God makes our next door neighbour.
G. K. Chesterton

♋

Money couldn't buy friends, but you get a
better class of enemy.
Spike Milligan

♋

Parents are the bones upon which children
sharpen their teeth.
Peter Ustinov

Old friends are best. King James used to call for his old shoes; they were easiest for his feet.
John Selden

♋

I believe that more unhappiness comes from this source than from any other – I mean from the attempt to prolong family connections unduly and to make people hang together artificially who would never naturally do so.
Samuel Butler

♋

Don't hold your parents up to contempt. After all, you are their son, and it is just possible that you may take after them.
Evelyn Waugh

## Families and Friends

I love children, especially when they cry for
then someone takes them away.
Nancy Mitford

☙

Honolulu – it's got everything. Sand for the
children, sun for the wife, sharks for the wife's
mother.
Ken Dodd

☙

Choose your companions carefully – you may
have to eat them.
W. C. Sellar (1898-1951) and R. J. Yeatman (1898-1968),
humourists

But there, everything has its drawbacks, as the man said when his mother-in-law died, and they came down upon him for the funeral expenses.
Jerome K. Jerome

Gentlemen with broad chests and ambitious intentions do sometimes disappoint their friends by failing to carry the world before them.
T. S. Eliot

The main purpose of children's parties is to remind you that there are children more awful than your own.
Katherine Whitehorn

Many a man who thinks to found a home discovers that he has merely opened a tavern for his friends.
Norman Douglas, novelist (1868-1952)

❦

My father was frightened of his mother. I was frightened of my father, and I'm damned well going to make sure that my children are frightened of me.
King George V (1865-1936)

❦

Friends are God's apology for relations.
Hugh Kingsmill, writer (1889-1949)

Children always assume the sexual lives of
their parents come to a grinding halt at their
conception.
Alan Bennett

ॐ

I have lost friends, some by death... others
through sheer inability to cross the street.
Virginia Woolf

ॐ

The family – that dear octopus from whose
tentacles we never quite escape.
Dodie Smith, dramatist (1896-1990)

Arthur: It's at times like this I wish I'd listened to my mother.
Ford: Why, what did she say?
Arthur: I don't know, I never listened.
Douglas Adams, *The Hitchhiker's Guide to the Galaxy*, (1979)

♋

Friends are thieves of time.
Francis Bacon

♋

It is a melancholy truth that even great men have their poor relations.
Charles Dickens, *Bleak House*, (1852-1853)

Mussolini… Mussolini is the only statesman who had the requisite courage to have his son-in-law executed.
Winston Churchill in response to his son-in-law's question as to who was the greatest statesman

☉

Before I got married I had six theories about bringing up children; now I have six children, and no theories.
John Wilmot, poet and writer (1647-1680)

☉

Wit is the salt of conversation, not the food.
William Hazlitt

My mother protected me from the world and
my father threatened me with it.
Quentin Crisp, *The Naked Civil Servant*, 1975

♋

If you must hold yourself up to your children
as an object lesson, hold yourself up as a
warning and not as an example.
George Bernard Shaw

♋

But of all plagues, good Heaven, thy wrath can
send,
Save me, oh, save me, from the candid friend!
George Canning, statesman (1770-1827)

I have a stepladder. It's a very nice stepladder but it's sad that I never knew my real ladder.
Craig Charles, actor

♋

I have never understood this liking for war. It panders to instincts already well catered for in any respectable domestic establishment.
Alan Bennett

♋

And if I have a child, he will be born horrifically deformed, but, after much hard work and management, will overcome his disabilities to become a serial killer.
Rob Newman defining pessimism

Where does the family start? It starts with a young man falling in love with a girl – no superior alternative has yet been found.
Winston Churchill

᪣

After all, what is a pedestrian? He is a man who has two cars – one being driven by his wife, the other by one of his children.
Robert Bradbury, City Official for Liverpool

᪣

It [is] gentlemanly to get one's questions very slightly wrong. In that way one unprigs oneself and allows the company to correct one.
Lord Ribblesdale, peer (1834-1925)

I've always been interested in people, but I've never liked them.
W. Somerset Maugham

The real art of conversation is not only to say the right thing in the right place but to leave unsaid the wrong thing at the tempting moment.
Lady Dorothy Nevill

It is a good rule in life never to apologise. The right sort of people don't want apologies, and the wrong sort take a mean advantage of them.
P. G. Wodehouse

Incessant company is as bad as solitary confinement.
Virginia Woolf

Dontopedology is the science of opening your mouth and putting your foot in it. I've been practising it for years.
Prince Philip, Duke of Edinburgh

There are three kinds of man you must never trust: a man who hunts south of the Thames, a man who has soup for lunch; and a man who waxes his moustache.
James Richards, architectural writer and critic quoting his father, *Memoirs of an Unjust Fella*, (1980)

The trouble with her is that she lacks the power of conversation but not the power of speech.
George Bernard Shaw

ം

I know I've got a degree. Why does that mean I have to spend my life with intellectuals? I've got a life-saving certificate but I don't spend my evenings diving for a rubber brick with my pyjamas on.
Victoria Wood

ം

A person who is keen to shake your hand usually has something up his sleeve.
Alec Guinness, actor (1914-2000)

Never say a humorous thing to a man who does not possess humour. He will always use it in evidence against you.
Herbert Beerbohm Tree

☙

The penalty for success is to be bored by the people who used to snub you.
Nancy Astor

☙

I am patient with stupidity but not with those who are proud of it.
Edith Sitwell

It is a common delusion that you make things better by talking about them.
Dame Rose Macaulay, novelist (1881-1958)

Unless one is a genius, it is best to aim at being intelligible.
Anthony Hope Hawkins

In my mind, there is nothing so illiberal and so ill-bred, as audible laughter.
Lord Chesterfield

The aim of a joke is not to degrade the human being but to remind him that he is already degraded.
George Orwell

♋

'Know thyself' is a most superfluous direction. We can't avoid it. We can only hope that no one else knows.
Ivy Compton-Burnett

♋

I am now a true idler and the thought of dancing on Ecstasy seems ridiculous – I'd much rather talk about Kent.
Will Self in interview with *The Idler*

Never seem more learned than the people you are with. Wear your learning like a pocket watch and keep it hidden. Do not pull it out to count the hours, but give the time when you are asked.
Lord Chesterfield

# Culture

All true histories contain instruction; though, in some, the treasure may be hard to find, and when found, so trivial in quantity that the dry, shrivelled kernel scarcely compensates for the trouble of cracking the nut.
Anne Brontë, novelist (1820-1849)

❥

No opera plot can be sensible, for in sensible situations people do not sing.
W. H. Auden, poet (1907-1973)

❥

It is extraordinary how potent cheap music is.
Noel Coward

The avoidance of taxes is the only intellectual pursuit that carries any reward.
John Maynard Keynes, economist (1883-1946)

Beethoven always sounds to me like the upsetting of a bag of nails, with here and there an also dropped hammer.
John Ruskin, writer (1819-1900)

The English are not very spiritual people, so they invented cricket to give them some idea of eternity.
George Bernard Shaw

The harpsichord sounds like two skeletons copulating on a corrugated iron roof – in a thunderstorm.
Thomas Beecham

♋

His vibrato sounded like he was driving a tractor over a ploughed field with weights tied to his scrotum.
Spike Milligan

♋

There are two golden rules for an orchestra: start together and finish together. The public doesn't give a damn what goes on in between.
Thomas Beecham

Television? Television is for being on, dear boy,
not watching.
Noel Coward

♋

Prince looks like a dwarf who's been dipped
in a bucket of pubic hair.
Boy George, musician

♋

I couldn't warm to Chuck Berry even if I was
cremated next to him.
Keith Richards, musician

Music-hall songs provide the dull with wit, just as proverbs provide them with wisdom.
W. Somerset Maugham

☞

Acting has been described as farting about in disguise.
Peter O'Toole

☞

People are wrong when they say that opera is not what it used to be. It *is* what it used to be. That is what is wrong with it.
Noel Coward

Rock and roll is a bit like Las Vegas: guys dressed up in their sisters' clothes pretending to be rebellious and angry but not really angry about anything.
Sting

♋

She has the look of a woman who has just dined off her husband.
Laurence Durrell, writer (1912-1990) on the Mona Lisa

♋

The remarkable thing about Shakespeare is that he really is very good, in spite of all the people who say he is very good.
Robert Graves

I think that a lifetime of listening to disco music is a high price to pay for one's sexual preference.
Quentin Crisp

♋

Skill without imagination is craftsmanship and gives us many useful objects such as wickerwork picnic baskets. Imagination without skill gives us modern art.
Tom Stoppard

♋

Education... has produced a vast population able to read but unable to distinguish what is worth reading.
G. M. Trevelyan, historian (1876-1962)

We are going to convene a summit with Damien Hirst and the rest of the gang, at which they are going to explain to the nation what it all means. Let us have a national 'mission to explain' by the Saatchi mob, which will be massively popular.
Boris Johnson's new manifesto as new Shadow Arts Minister

♋

The people of Crete unfortunately make more history than they can consume locally.
Saki

♋

Manchester produces what to me is the *Pickwick Papers*. That is to say *Coronation Street*. Mondays and Wednesdays, I live for them. Thank God, half past seven tonight and I shall be in paradise.
John Betjeman, poet (1906-1984)

If Botticelli were alive today he'd be working for Vogue.
Peter Ustinov

☙

I want to do a musical movie. Like Evita, but with good music.
Elton John

☙

Art consists of limitation. The most beautiful part of every picture is the frame.
G. K. Chesterton

☙

It's strange that people don't recognise the enormous decline in taste melody, rhythm, harmony and invention since the days of Elvis, Chuck Berry and The Beatles.
Roger Scruton, philosopher, *The Independent*, 24/01/2001

# Life

Life is as tedious as a twice-told tale
Vexing the dull ear of a drowsy man.
William Shakespeare, *King John*

My meaning in saying he is a good man, is to
have you understand me that he is sufficient.
William Shakespeare, *The Merchant of Venice*

Never forget that only dead fish swim with
the stream.
Malcolm Muggeridge, *Radio Times*, 09/07/1964

Drama is life with the dull bits cut out.
Alfred Hitchcock

🦀

Don't be afraid to take big steps. You can't cross a chasm in two small jumps.
David Lloyd George

🦀

It is always the best policy to tell the truth, unless, of course, you are an exceptionally good liar.
Jerome K. Jerome

Blessed is the man, who having nothing to say, abstains from giving wordy evidence of the fact.
George Eliot

♋

If you can't be a good example, then you'll just have to be a horrible warning.
Catherine Aird, author

♋

He's simply got the instinct for being unhappy highly developed.
Saki

Better keep your mouth shut and be thought a fool than open it and remove all doubt.
Denis Thatcher, husband of former Prime Minister Margaret Thatcher (1915-2003)

∽

If you are cast in a different mould to the majority, it is no merit of yours: Nature did it.
Charlotte Brontë, novelist (1816-1855)

∽

Sometimes one likes foolish people for their folly, better than wise people for their wisdom.
Mrs Elizabeth Gaskell, novelist (1810-1865)

When all is said and done, monotony may after all be the best condition for creation.
Margaret Sackville, poet (1876-1963)

It is dangerous to be sincere unless you are also stupid.
George Bernard Shaw

My school days were the happiest days of my life; which should give you some indication of the misery I've endured over the past twenty-five years.
Paul Merton

Something is always wrong, Balders. The fact that I am not a millionaire aristocrat with the sexual capacity of a rutting rhino is a constant niggle.
*Blackadder*

♋

Pessimism… is, in brief, playing the sure game. You cannot lose at it; you may gain. It is the only view of life in which you can never be disappointed.
Thomas Hardy, *Jude the Obscure* 1895

♋

The important thing when you are going to do something brave is to have someone on hand to witness it.
Michael Howard, MC, Professor of the History of War, Oxford

Man prefers to believe what he prefers to be true.
Francis Bacon

Discretion is the polite word for hypocrisy.
Christine Keeler, model

Life is like a tin of sardines. We are all looking for the key.
Alan Bennett

Fame is like ice cream. It's only bad if you eat too much.
Mick Jagger

🅖

You should make a point of trying every experience once, excepting incest and folk-dancing.
Arnold Bax, composer (1883-1953), quoting an anonymous Scotsman

🅖

The only man who wasn't spoiled by being lionised was Daniel.
Herbert Beerbohm Tree

One of the universal rules of happiness is: always be wary of any helpful item that weighs less than its operating manual.
Terry Pratchett

The power of accurate observation is commonly called cynicism by those who have not got it.
George Bernard Shaw

The place where optimism most flourishes is the lunatic asylum.
Havelock Ellis

Life's incredibly boring. I don't say that in an effort to seem vaguely amusing but the secret of life is that there's no secret, it's just exceedingly boring.
Morrissey, musician

One might well say that mankind is divisible into two great classes: hosts and guests.
Max Beerbohm

You have to be a bastard to make it, and that's a fact. And the Beatles are the biggest bastards on earth.
John Lennon

For what do we live, but to make sport for our
neighbours, and laugh at them in our turn?
Jane Austen

For what do we live, but to make sport for our

Reality leaves a lot to the imagination.
John Lennon

Life is a wretched grey Saturday, but it has to
be lived through.
Anthony Burgess

# Animals

Monkeys, who very sensibly refrain from speech, lest they should be set to earn their living.
Kenneth Grahame, author (1859-1932)

You will find that the woman who is really kind to dogs is always one who has failed to inspire sympathy in men.
Max Beerbohm, *Zuleika Dobson,* 1911

To his dog, every man is Napoleon; hence the constant popularity of dogs.
Aldous Huxley

To his dog, every man is Napoleon; hence the
constant popularity of dogs.
Aldous Huxley

Histories are more full of examples of the fidelity of dogs than of friends.
Alexander Pope

The trouble with cats is that they've got no tact.
P. G. Wodehouse

# Animals

Biologically speaking, if something bites you it's more likely to be female.
Desmond Morris, scientist

Bloke on TV who goes on about how bloody great animals are all the time. He forgets that it wasn't an animal who invented the TV or the safari suit.
David Baddiel, comedian on David Attenborough

You have no control over your cat! You can't say to your cat 'Cat! Heel! Stay – wait! Lie down – roll over!' 'Cos the cat would just be sitting there going, 'Interesting words... have you finished?'
Eddie Izzard

Animals are such agreeable friends – they ask
no questions, they pass no criticisms.
George Eliot

❧

Fox-terriers are born with about four times as
much original sin in them as other dogs.
Jerome K. Jerome

❧

A horse is dangerous at both ends and
uncomfortable in the middle.
Ian Fleming

# Animals

The early bird may get the worm, but it's the second mouse that gets the cheese.
Jeremy Paxman, presenter of political shows

♋

No human being, however great, or powerful, was ever so free as a fish.
John Ruskin

♋

While Darwinian Man, though well-behaved. At best is only a monkey shaved!
W. S. Gilbert

Man is Nature's sole mistake.
W. S. Gilbert

♋

One of the main arguments in favour of fox hunting is that foxes kill chickens. But so does Bernard Matthews and nobody advocates chasing him across the country with a pack of dogs and tearing him to pieces.
Alexi Sayle

♋

I have often had the impression that, to penguins, man is just another penguin – different, less predictable, occasionally violent, but tolerable company when he sits still and minds his own business.
Bernard Stonehouse, penguinologist

# Animals

You never see animals going through the absurd and often horrible fooleries of magic and religion... Dogs do not ritually urinate in the hope of persuading heaven to do the same and send down rain. Asses do not bray a liturgy to cloudless skies. Nor do cats attempt, by abstinence from cat's meat, to wheedle the feline spirits into benevolence. Only man behaves with such gratuitous folly. It is the price he has to pay for being intelligent but not, as yet, quite intelligent enough.
Aldous Huxley

♋

If a dog jumps into your lap it is because he is fond of you; but if a cat does the same thing it is because your lap is warmer.
Alfred North Whitehead, mathematician (1861–1947)

The London Zoo is an animal microcosm of London, and even the lions, as a rule, behave as if they had been born in South Kensington.
Leonard Woolf, novelist and editor (1880-1969)

If you think you're too small to have an impact, try going to bed with a mosquito in the room.
Anita Roddick, businesswoman, founder of The Body Shop

# Death

Dying is a very dull, dreary affair. And my advice to you is to have nothing whatever to do with it.
W. Somerset Maugham

My aunt died at precisely 10:47 am and the old grandfather clock stopped precisely at this moment also.  It fell on her.
Paul Merton

At my age I do what Mark Twain did. I get my daily paper, look at the obituaries page and if I'm not there I carry on as usual.
Patrick Moore

♋

There is nothing quite so good as burial at sea. It is simple, tidy, and not very incriminating.
Alfred Hitchcock

♋

I'd like to go there. But if Jeffrey Archer is there I want to go to Lewisham.
Spike Milligan on heaven

I shall not waste my days in trying to prolong them.
Ian Fleming

❧

Be happy while you're living, for you're a long time dead.
Scottish Proverb

❧

Death seems to provide the minds of the Anglo-Saxon race with a greater fund of amusement than any other single subject.
Dorothy L. Sayers

Autobiography: an obituary in serial form with the last instalment missing.
Quentin Crisp

♋

I am ready to meet my Maker. Whether my Maker is prepared for the great ordeal of meeting me is another matter.
Winston Churchill

♋

If this is dying, then I don't think much of it.
Lytton Strachey

# Death

Death comes along like a gas bill one can't pay.
Anthony Burgess

🦀

Eternity is a terrible thing. I mean, where's it going to end?
Tom Stoppard

🦀

The most convenient time to tax rich people.
David Lloyd George on death

'There's been an accident!' they said,
'Your servant's cut in half; he's dead!'
'Indeed!' said Mr Jones, 'and please
Send me the half that's got my keys'
Harry Graham, poet (1874-1936), *Ruthless Rhymes*

I am told he makes a very handsome corpse,
and becomes his coffin prodigiously.
Oliver Goldsmith

Man is the only animal that can remain on
friendly terms with the victims he intends to
eat until he eats them.
Samuel Butler

# Death

They announced on US TV that Patrick MacNee, star of *The Avengers*, had died. So they rang up my daughter in Palm Springs. 'Sorry to hear that your father's dead.' She said: 'But I was talking to him 12 minutes ago in Australia.' They said, 'No, he's dead – it's just the time difference.'
Patrick MacNee, actor

♋

Waldo is one of those people who would be enormously improved by death.
Saki

♋

I blame myself for my boyfriend's death. I shot him.
Jo Brand

This is the first age that's paid much attention
to the future, which is a little ironic since we
may not have one.
Arthur C. Clarke

Something which everyone reaches at the rate
of sixty minutes an hour.
C. S. Lewis on the future

If you do not think about your future, you
cannot have one.
John Galsworthy, author (1867-1933)

Birth was the death of him.
Samuel Beckett, playwright (1906-1989)

# Fashion and Beauty

Fashions, after all, are only induced epidemics.
George Bernard Shaw, *The Doctor's Dilemma*, (1906)

♋

A fashion is merely a form of ugliness so unbearable that we are compelled to alter it every six months.
Oscar Wilde, quoted in Richard Ellmann's *Oscar Wilde,* 1987: Richard Ellmann, critic and biographer (1918-1987)

♋

Taste does not come by chance: it is a long and laborious task to acquire it.
Joshua Reynolds, painter (1723-1792)

♋

If you are not in fashion, you are nobody.
Lord Chesterfield, *Letter to his Son*, April 30, 1750

♋

There's never a new fashion but it's old.
Geoffrey Chaucer, *The Canterbury Tales*

Good taste is the worst vice ever invented.
Dame Edith Sitwell

๛

Custom will reconcile people to any atrocity; and fashion will drive them to acquire any custom.
William Shakespeare *The Tragedy of Richard III*

๛

The novelties of one generation are only the resuscitated fashions of the generation before last
George Bernard Shaw

Women thrive on novelty and are easy meat for the commerce of fashion. Men prefer old pipes and torn jackets.
Anthony Burgess

♋

She looked as if she'd been poured into her clothes and had forgotten to say when.
P. G. Wodehouse

♋

I wouldn't dream of taking life as it comes: it may not be colour-coordinated.
Julian Clary, entertainer

# Fashion and Beauty

The fashion wears out more apparel than the man.
William Shakespeare, *Much Ado About Nothing*

∞

Manners are especially the need of the plain. The pretty can get away with anything.
Evelyn Waugh

∞

I'd like to think that no professional stylist would do this for him. It's kitsch, but surely not deliberately so.
Nicky Clarke, hair stylist on David Seaman's ponytail

Basically rock stardom comes down to the cut of your trousers.
David Bowie, musician

☞

I have a face that is a cross between two pounds of halibut and an explosion in an old-clothes closet. If it isn't mobile, it's dead.
David Niven, actor

☞

As you run around Battersea Park in them, looking like a cross between a member of the SAS and Blake's Seven, there is always the lingering fear of arrest.
Brian Moore, rugby player in 1995 on the England rugby

I'm so gorgeous, there's a six month waiting list for birds to suddenly appear, every time I am near!
Cat from *Red Dwarf*

[Your] horrid image doth unfix my hair.
William Shakespeare, *Macbeth*

I'm all for killing animals and turning them into handbags. I just don't want to have to eat them.
Victoria Wood

Never trust a man who, when left alone in a room with a tea cosy, doesn't try it on.
Billy Connolly

♋

Fallacies do not cease to be fallacies because they become fashions.
G. K. Chesterton

♋

The sense of being well-dressed gives a feeling of inward tranquillity which religion is powerless to bestow.
Miss C. F. Forbes, writer (1817-1911)

If it were the fashion to go naked, the face would be hardly observed.
Lady Wortley Montagu

❥

Beauty when most unclothed is clothed best.
Phineas Fletcher, poet (1584-1650), *Sicelides*, 1614

❥

I always say beauty is only sin deep.
Saki